11
C.y
to

David Shelton

EYES OF THE TAILLESS ANIMALS

Mr David Shelton
5808 Lance Dr
Kokomo IN 46902-5491

Prison Memoirs of a

North Korean Woman

Soon Ok Lee

Living Sacrifice Book Company
Bartlesville, OK

Eyes of the Tailless Animals:
Prison Memoirs of a North Korean Woman

Living Sacrifice Book Company
P.O. Box 2273
Bartlesville, OK 74005-2273

© 1999, Soon Ok Lee. All rights reserved. No part of this book may be reproduced, stored in a retrieval system, or transmitted in any form or by any means, except in the case of brief quotations printed in articles or reviews, without prior permission in writing from the publisher.

Originally published as *Kori Upnen Gymseung Deuleui Noonbit*, © 1996, Chunji Media (Seoul).

Translated by Rev. Bahn-Suk Lee and Jin Young Choi
Design and production by Genesis Group
Cover by David Marty Design
Sketches by Grace Kwon
Printed in the United States of America

Unless otherwise indicated, Scripture quotations are taken from the *New King James* version, © 1979, 1980, 1982 by Thomas Nelson Inc., Publishers, Nashville, Tennessee.

Library of Congress Cataloging-in-Publication Data
Yi, Sun-ok, 1947–
    [832, kkori omnun chimsungdul ui nunpit. English]
    Eyes of the tailless animals : prison memoirs of a North Korean woman /
Soon Ok Lee ; [translated by Rev. Bahn-Suk Lee and Jin Young Choi].
        p. cm.
    ISBN 0-88264-335-5 (pbk.)
    1. Yi, Sun-ok, 1947– 2. Women prisoners—Korea (North)—Biography.
3. Prisons—Korea (North) 4. Communism and Christianity—Korea (North)
I. Title: Originally published as: Kori upnen gymseung deuleui noonbit. II. Title.

HV9815.6.Y5 1999
365'.45'092—dc21
[B]
                                                                99-047863

CONTENTS

FOREWORD

IN THESE PAGES, MRS. SOON OK LEE describes a "hopeless" world. Yet do we hope in God and His salvation because of the good things we see around us? In Romans 8:24, the apostle Paul states that "we are saved by hope: but hope that is seen is not hope" (KJV).

When I first read the story of Mrs. Lee, I found it to be one of the most chilling manuscripts I had ever read. Then, when I met her, I saw the face of one in whom God dwells—a face with hope. The North Korea she describes still maintains a brutal godless system. I know; I was recently there. It is one of the 14 nations where I have visited brothers and sisters in the persecuted church.

I could never have vicariously received even a tiny part of Mrs. Lee's life story without the knowledge, the hope, that there is a godly judgment and that there is eternal life. Knowing this, the sparkling diamond that is Christ, and seeing that diamond shine even in this brutal concentration camp system causes me to reaffirm that rags or riches, sickness or health, it is only Christ, only Christ that truly will sustain us and carry us.

And what about North Koreans who are not in labor camps but walk "freely" in the streets of their prison nation? The ones I met were hungry for God. Fifty years of brainwashing did not succeed. As Richard Wurmbrand once said, "There is something more powerful than brainwashing—it is called heartwashing." A North Korean man I encountered on my recent trip silently accepted a Christian book, watching carefully to see that the others in his party did not observe. The next morning he whispered excitedly, "I stayed up until three a.m. reading! I always wanted to have my own Christian book. Can you get me any more?" This is the true power that will survive in North Korea, not their missiles or their gangster leaders who starve their people.

Tens of millions of dollars are spent maintaining the body of the dead leader Kim Il Sung. I viewed his body in a huge mausoleum located on hundreds of acres. The body of my leader, Jesus Christ, is not in a mausoleum. He arose to shed hope in the lives of mankind everywhere.

It is my prayer that as you read this book, your hope in Christ will deepen and your love for the country of North Korea will burn with a heavenly passion, desiring to see all come to Christ.

"Now may the God of hope fill you with all joy and peace in believing, that you may abound in hope by the power of the Holy Spirit" (Romans 15:13). "For surely there is a hereafter, and your hope will not be cut off" (Proverbs 23:18).

Come quickly, Lord Jesus!

TOM WHITE
USA Director, The Voice of the Martyrs

Special thanks to…
Chunji Media in Seoul
Cornerstone Ministries and Rev. Bahn-Suk Lee
Jin Young Choi
Cheryl Odden and VOM Communications
Lynn Copeland
Joette Whims
Betty Slonczewski

Chapter 1

OUT OF THE DEN OF DEATH

EVEN NOW, IT IS HARD TO BELIEVE that I am still alive. When I walk in the streets, sit, or sleep in South Korea, the vision of where I had been overwhelms me. The place where I was confined was not a place that normal people can imagine. It was a den of death. It was a place where the wardens demanded that you leave your humanness behind when you entered the doors.

My life began as one of privilege and hope. I was born in 1947 in Chungjin City, North Korea. I was an only child in a family that was well off by the Communist country's standard. My grandfather had served in the army in the northern part of Manchuria. When Korea was a colony of Japan, my father fought for Korea's independence along with Kim Il Sung, who became the dictator of North Korea. My grandfather and father were honored men.

From my birth, I was married to the Communist party. Since there has not been a son in the family for four generations, I was thoroughly trained under the Communist doctrine. As a child of patriarchs, I received special treatment and attended the prestigious People's Economic College. After I graduated, my parents helped me enter the Noh-dong Party, which is the Communist labor party. I was assigned as a supervisor of the material distribution center and was considered one of the most successful women.

Every moment, awake or asleep, I devoted to the Party. I never questioned the Party's doctrine, but accepted it as absolute fact. I worked for the government with all my heart, soul, and strength.

My family moved to Onsung County during the war between North and South Korea. There I graduated from Ra-Hueng mechanical industrial high school in 1963 and entered the economic, technical college. After graduating with a business degree, I obtained a license as an accountant, and in 1969 I began working as a supervisor in the commercial department of Onsung County. In 1978, I became head of the Onsung County officer's distribution material center. It was rare for a woman in her early twenties to be a member of the Noh-dong Party and to head an office. In Onsung County, I was the only one.

My husband, who was seven years older than I am, was a teacher. His family was also considered good Communists. In his mid-twenties, he became principal of the middle school and high school, which is a rare occurrence in North Korea.

We had one son, Kim Dong Chel. I knew he was smart from an early age, and he knew how to respect his elders. When he was sixteen, he worked as a national security guard, and two years later, he worked for the military police outside a political prison camp. He passed the competitive entrance exam for Kim Il Sung University, the most prestigious university in North Korea. My husband and I were very proud of him. As a family, all our wishes had come true; we were so happy. Then the cloud of unhappiness began to overshadow our lives.

Interrogation and Prison

My misery began after I returned from a business trip to China. I had gone there to buy fabric for officers of the government department and the Communist Party. One officer of North Korea's Public Security Bureau (much like Russia's KGB) asked me for more fabric for a suit than was his share. I could not do what he asked because my supplies were limited. Because I refused to satisfy his greed, I was thrown into the dark world of the prison system. I was cruelly and terribly punished.

During fourteen months of interrogation, I endured tremendous physical and mental pain. As a frail woman, I could hardly bear it. After experiencing all kinds of threats, torture, appeasement, and deceptions, I was sentenced to thirteen years of imprisonment in a resocialization center. People who do not obey the rules of the government are sent there.

All my life I had been told that North Korea's communism values every human being. Yet I could not believe what I saw in that horrible place in my country. None of the prisoners were allowed to talk, laugh, sing, or look in a mirror. They had to sit on their knees with their heads bowed and answer questions when an interrogator spoke. Prisoners had to work eighteen hours a day at hard labor. If they did not complete their work for that day, they were thrown into solitary confinement.

The prison was a place where the "animals that do not have tails" lived. That is what the prisoners were. It is beyond human comprehension how the Communist Party could treat people this way. How can the Communist system, in the time of no war, contradict its teachings by torturing people who share the same bloodline?

Miraculous Freedom

In December 1992, I walked out of the prison's heavy door in Khechen, North Korea. God had provided a miracle, one that had not happened in thirty years. From the first, I wanted to tell everyone about the prisons and the people I left behind. I did not want to be quiet about what I had endured and seen.

The moment I stepped into South Korea, I craved the opportunity to speak my mind. I wanted to shout out all the anger and sorrow I had accumulated from the humiliation, the scornful treatment, and the forced silence of my years in North Korean prisons. I wanted to gather the lamentations of thousands and millions of prisoners who live under conditions humans cannot bear, especially my brothers and sisters in the Lord. I wanted to proclaim on their behalf, "We're human beings too. We have a right to speak!"

After I defected, I found God, and am able to praise Him freely. I am so happy. No words could describe my happiness. Even now as I look back, I see where God led me and the miracles He did on my behalf.

Pleading Eyes

I did not defect to South Korea solely for my own happiness. I also have a responsibility to those who are still in prison. I cannot forget about them. When I walked out of that place, I saw the eyes of the six thousand "tailless animals" I left behind. I felt their eyes pleading, "You who leave here alive must witness to the people outside about our lives in prison." Their keen eyes compelled me to write about their situation.

Whenever I got tired, I remembered their eyes and kept writing.

Today when I hear about the desperate food shortage in North Korea, my heart breaks. If people outside the prison are starving, I cannot imagine how people inside the prison are being treated and what kind of pain they are going through. And Christians are suffering the most.

It is nice to send rice to North Korea and to negotiate with the North Korean government to help them solve their food and economic problems. But more important than rice is to send the love of God to them. North Korea has a great history of Christianity. Hundreds of thousands of believers once worshipped there. Yet today there are many hungry, dying people in North Korea who need not only food for their bodies, but also the Bread of Life, Jesus Christ.

Let me begin my story and their story by telling how I came to be in the den of death.

Chapter 2

THE DEN OF EVILS

ON OCTOBER 26, 1986, I WAS enjoying a peaceful morning at work when tragedy struck. It was on a Sunday in which Korean women make *kim chi*, Korean pickles, for the winter. At my office, all was quiet because the women in the other departments had the day off. Because I was responsible for counting the inventory and preparing a report on purchase orders and the distribution of goods, I had come to work. I planned to work in the morning and rest all afternoon. To finish earlier, I told the planning department chief to take messages for me if the telephone rang.

As I was working, I heard an automobile horn honking loudly. Curious, I opened the window and looked outside. I noticed an army security bureau chief's car out in the building yard. Surprised that the car was here on Sunday, I wondered, *What brought him out here when everyone is off for the day?* Since the warehouse was closed, no one was available to give him any material. Without thinking much more, I closed the window and sat back down at my desk and continued working.

A few minutes later, Chen Yung Gen, a public security inspection chief, came into my office. He said, "The bureau chief is out in the alley, and he wants to talk to you."

The thought crossed my mind, *If he has something to say to me, he should have come into the office. Why does this man take such a humble position? He is so much more important than I am.*

11

The police officer pushed me onto the train.

The inspection chief urged, "This will take only a few minutes, so let's go down."

A Frightening Twenty Minutes

I went with him without straightening the papers on my desk. As soon as we reached the car, the inspection chief snarled, "Get in the car." He pushed me inside and slammed the door behind me.

Before I realized what was going on, the car took off. Within minutes, we pulled up to the back door of the Onsung train station near where the freight is handled. Behind the platform was a train that had arrived on the line from Ra-Jin to Pyongyang.

Events had happened so quickly that I didn't even have time to think. I was pulled out of the car and pushed roughly onto the train.

I finally found my voice and yelled, "What's the matter? Why are you doing this?"

The chief put his hand over my mouth and spit out a command, "Shut up! Once you get up there, you'll find out."

Someone shoved me into one of the compartments on the train. The compartment had room for four people. Two public security officers in street clothes were waiting for me. The inspection chief gave them a sign with his eyes and handed me off to them. Before I knew what was happening, the train left Onsung station and passed over the bridge.

It had taken only twenty minutes from the time I left my office to the moment I was pushed into the train compartment. As the saying goes, the soy beans were cooked at the speed of lightning. The whole incident had obviously been preplanned.

At the Hwe-Ryung station, Kim Dong Su entered the train compartment. I had known him for many years; however, he didn't say anything to me. When mealtime arrived, he told the other two agents to go into another compartment to eat. After they left, he began to speak. "I feel so bad I can hardly look at you. I think of you as an older sister, and now you may hate me for doing this. I am just doing what my boss ordered me to do."

Kim Dong Su explained what had happened that morning. When he arrived at work, he was summoned by the bureau chief and given an order: "Go arrest Soon Ok Lee who is working at the distribution center and bring her to the interrogation center." His orders were to deliver me to the agents in the compartment. Then the chief cautioned, "Dong Su, keep her away from the public while she is on the train. No one is allowed to come into the compartment and talk to her." Kim Dong Su advised me to be ready for what was to come and to not try to commit suicide.

A little later the guards returned, and Kim Dong Su stopped talking to me. Sensitive to his position, I closed my eyes.

The guards pulled out Chinese filter cigarettes and hard liquor. After they finished drinking, they began talking to each other. They said that the bureau chief had especially prepared them for their service. They talked about the importance of the job they were doing for him. If they completed their assignment, he would treat them well and give them gifts. Through their conversation, I began to understand my situation.

The Circumstances of My Arrest

The circumstances of my arrest began in the fall of 1985. Kim Jong Il, the son of North Korea's dictator, used to wear a casual jacket on official occasions which became a very popular style among Party officers. The jacket was made from a special fabric that was not produced in North Korea, so I had to travel to China to purchase 1,200 yards to meet the demands.

My responsibility was to distribute the material to all the officers in Onsung County. However, at that time, the North Korean economic situation was not good. When I needed 100 yards to distribute, I had only 80. My job became a headache. Some officers asked me for more than their share, but I could not give it to them. I had to be fair. So sometimes I had to convince these people that I couldn't satisfy their requests and try to work out all the difficulties.

The security bureau chief asked to have two jackets made out of the fabric while everyone else received only one. Without raising my voice, I explained to him that I could not give him more than his share. Suddenly, he turned around and spit out, "All right, Soon Ok. You will regret this," and he left my office.

A few months after he got mad at me, I was arrested secretly and accused of two counts: violating the commercial policies of the Party and taking bribes. It didn't make any sense to me—I was as pure as snow. I had never committed either violation. It was all the security bureau chief's cunning scheme for revenge. The security bureau chief didn't have a permit from the Communist Party to arrest me. The deed was done through the public security bureau independent of the Communist Party.

To make things worse, my arrest became part of a conflict between the Public Security Bureau and the Noh-dong Party. Each group was trying to determine who was the most powerful. Obviously, when the Party found out about my situation, they insisted that I be released. However, because the security bureau had already reported the arrest to the highest ranking officers, they would have had to admit that I had done nothing wrong—which would have made them lose face.

So the security bureau tried every way to hold me. Before my arrest, the Central Communist Party discovered the security chief's illegal behavior and wanted to remove him from his post. Instead, the security chief falsely accused me to try to cover his illegal activities so he could save his own neck. He deviously planned my entire arrest. My situation became known as "the Onsung 65th incident" because I worked at the 65th distribution material distribution center. Soon everyone in North Korea knew about the incident, and the details of my arrest were used in retraining people in communism.

The First Prison Cell

The train ran for seven hours and finally arrived in Chungjin City where a car was waiting for me and the guards. I had no idea where the car was heading. After traveling for a while, the car stopped before a building with a large iron door. The driver signaled to a guard, and the heavy door opened. Inside I saw a small two-story building with iron bars on every window. I immediately guessed it must be a prison. The security guards took me to a reception area where a major and the public bureau inspection chief for that province were waiting for us. The major looked me over and said, "I got a telephone call that your group had left Onsung County's security bureau. Is this the woman?"

The inspection chief nodded.

A little later, a woman brought me into a room to search me. She confiscated my watch and grumbled, "It's so cold. Why aren't you wearing more clothing? Your nice clothes are not appropriate for someone who will be on the ground." She was treating me like a criminal and putting me down with her words. This was all a nightmare. She ripped off my buttons and zippers. *Maybe she thinks I could use them to hurt myself,* I thought. During the entire search, I felt so confused and shocked that I couldn't resist or defend myself.

Finally, I began to realize that something had gone terribly wrong. I felt dizzy. What in the world had I done wrong? Why was everyone treating me this way? Because I had never experienced anything this traumatic before, my mind and heart were in terrible pain.

After she finished the search, the woman took me back to the registration office. I was so weak, I could barely follow her. As I entered the office, Kim Dong Su stared at me silently. The major ordered, "Let's go to the jail cell," and began to drag me away. Kim Dong Su called after me, "Don't worry too much."

When we got to the cell block, the major showed me into an empty cell and threw me two tattered blankets. They were so thin that the two together wouldn't equal half a normal blanket. They smelled so badly of sweat and mildew that I could not even touch them.

That night, I sat up all night without sleeping. In the morning, I was given a breakfast of yellowish corn rice and a salty soup. I did not touch it because I had never eaten such poor food before. I didn't feel like eating anyway, so I just closed my eyes and thought about my situation. The days and nights crawled by until three days had passed. Still, no one came to get me.

After seven days, the guards took me to a room on the second floor. Sitting at a desk were the inspection chief from Onsung County and an agent. They ordered me to sit on a chair in the corner. The inspection chief began by saying, "We are inspecting the distribution at the 65th material distribution office. We're auditing all the operations. The inspectors responsible for the audit are myself and Hak Nam Kim, who is the province security bureau inspection agent."

What he said didn't make sense, so I replied, "I will not cooperate with this inspection because the county audit was completed on March 29. That audit was done incorrectly, and another inspection was already done. It's not legal to do three inspections on the same department. If you can show me a North Korean law that allows this, then I will agree." With those words, I figured I had clearly stated my position. (Until that time, I believed that the security bureau strictly followed North Korean laws. I did not know that they often illegally used their authority to commit wrongful acts against the people.)

Because I challenged him, the inspection chief retorted, "You'd better think again." Then he turned me over to Hak Nam Kim and went out.

The Interrogation Begins

After the inspection chief had gone, Hak Nam Kim, who was just twenty-eight years old and eleven years younger than me, said, "We left you alone for a week to think about why you are here. Have you figured it out? Unless you confess all your crimes, do not even think about walking out of here alive. I am a young, powerful officer, and I will show you what I can really do. Now that you are here, you will follow our way of doing things."

With that, he dragged me downstairs and pushed me through a door into a room containing about twenty to thirty men. As soon as I entered, I heard the men talking and a few ran over and threw a blanket over my head. They began to kick me. This happened so suddenly that I didn't even have time to scream. I felt like I was going to suffocate under the blanket. The kicks coming from everywhere were so hard that I began to see red and blue stars, sparkling brightly. Then I lost consciousness and fell to the floor.

I don't know how long the men kicked me and stomped on me, but when I awoke in my cell, my body ached so badly that I could not even move a finger. I felt as if every bone in my body were broken. The pain was indescribable.

A few hours later, Hak Nam Kim opened the door and said, "How did you like your introduction? Do you see what it is like here?" Then he shouted, "Get up right now!" But I was in so much pain I couldn't move. He yelled, "You have not really tasted our greeting, b——!" That is a terrible word to call anyone.

He called to two men from outside the room who came in and grabbed my arms. They dragged me like an animal on a rope, my feet dragging behind me. They took me back to the second floor to the same room I had been in earlier.

Then the interrogation really began. Hak Nam Kim and the inspection chief took turns questioning me twenty-four hours a day. For three days they did not let me close my eyes. They kept asking questions about what I had given to whom, the number of bribes I had received from government officials, what I distributed to whom after returning from China, which Communist Party and security bureau officials had gotten more than their share. Because I had been born in North Korea and was an educated person, I never thought I'd ever face a violation of my human rights or a criminal interrogation. But they kept beating me and demanding that I answer their questions. Soon I had gone so long without sleep that I couldn't understand what they were asking. I just kept repeating, "What do you want from me? I don't really understand." I was sure that they would release me because I hadn't done anything wrong.

I still didn't realize that I was the sacrificial lamb for the Onsung County security bureau. Kim Dum Jun, the assistant security inspection chief; Kim Hung Chung, the inspection section chief; and Chen Yung Gen, the public security inspection chief, were all working together. They accused me of violating the national property embezzlement law. If I didn't confess, they would send me to the rehabilitation center. If I confessed, that would cover up the illegal inspections done by the county's security bureau. If the Communist Party officials learned about the chief's illegal activities, they might relocate him for the wrong things he had done. Yet it still never occurred to me that they planned my arrest, the preliminary interrogation, and my transfer to the rehabilitation center.

The Torture Intensifies

The degree of torture and interrogation that I endured worsened. About 150 yards from the assembly area was a place where bricks were baked. The bricks are put inside a furnace and the entrance covered up. Once the bricks are baked, the entrance is opened. Sparks and dust cover the whole inside of the furnace.

One day, I had to endure the furnace as part of my interrogation. Guards pushed me in, and it was so hot inside that I couldn't breathe. Sparks hit me and thick smoke suffocated me until I fainted. They brought me out and dumped a bucket of cold water over my head to bring me back to consciousness. Then they took me back to the preliminary interrogation room and began asking the same questions over and over again. Hak Nam Kim screamed at me, "B———, put your fingerprints on the form. Sign here and then you can live!"

Day by day, the level of interrogation increased in intensity. Sometimes the eyes of Hak Nam Kim and the inspection chief looked like those of ravenous animals, shining with an unearthly light. It scared me to look into their eyes.

One day I was taken to another room. Hak Nam Kim put me on a chair on my knees and belted me to the chair. He stripped off all my clothes and began to lash me with a leather whip. I tried to move my leg to shield my body from the blows, but I was too tightly bound to the chair.

As he beat me, he screamed, "We will see, b———, how long you will survive. Until you put your fingerprints on the statement, don't even think you are going to get out of this place alive." His voice was evil. He hit me and he spit, and hit me even harder. I began to realize that after

I was suspended in the air from a bar.

being interrogated so severely, I would not get out of this place easily. I had to find some way of being strong moment by moment as I was tortured.

In the assembly area were three interrogation rooms. Each was used for a different type of torture. In one room, they fettered my hands to the bars on the window of the door and my feet to metal near the bottom. As my body was suspended in the air, the flesh in my legs felt like it was being cut off.

The torturers took a leather whip and began to hit me all over. First my flesh puffed up, then my skin peeled off and my whole body became bloody. As the beating continued, the pain dulled. But my whole body swelled so badly that my arms and legs looked like fat trees. I could not bend over or sit down, and had to stand even when using the toilet.

Still, I resisted Hak Nam Kim, saying, "I cannot sign the written statement because it is not true."

My refusal angered Hak Nam Kim, so he made me endure even worse kinds of torture. He took me from one interrogation room to another.

One day the men took off my clothes so they could torture me. Even worse than the pain of the torture was being totally naked in front of all these men. The shame of it pounded in my ears. I was so angry I fought them.

One man hit me so hard in the face that I lost consciousness. When I woke up, I felt something in my mouth. It was broken teeth. My nose and mouth had bled so much that the floor was a bloody sea. My face was covered in blood and was so swollen around my eyes that I could not see. I could barely open my lips to spit out my four broken teeth. Many of the other teeth had been knocked loose and my gums were swollen. The pain was so severe that I thought all my teeth would drop out.

These interrogations often began at 5 a.m. and lasted until midnight when I was brought back to my prison cell. My tormentors kept threatening me and torturing me to get me to sign the false statement and asking those same questions over and over. I didn't want to lose consciousness because I was afraid I would slip and admit to something I didn't do. After a while, I found ways to survive the torture.

Like Frozen Fish

As time passed and winter arrived, I still had not signed the statement.

Hak Nam Kim raved at me, "B——, you must be so comfortable in your warm room that you keep resisting. You need to learn your lesson!" He took all my clothes except my underwear, then led me outside the building into the prison yard. He commanded the guard, "Let this woman freeze."

The winter night temperature was cold enough to freeze human flesh. For the first twenty or thirty minutes, my hands and feet were so cold that I felt kind of crazy. After that came the pain. But soon the pain disappeared and my body became numb.

Beginning in January, I was sent out into the cold for one hour every night. The prison guards called this the frozen fish torture.

Since my arrival at the farmer's assembly place, my interrogators had segregated me from the other prisoners. For months I did not know who was in the prison camp or how many prisoners it contained. But at the end of the month when I was placed in the yard for my frozen-fish torture, I saw about ten male prisoners and one woman who were lined up on their knees. The guards ordered me to sit at the end of the line. As I was passing by the men, I heard a very low voice whisper, "Comrade Soon Ok." I looked at who could have said my name and saw Choi Young Hwan, who used to be the manager of the commercial office of Hweleng Yung Province. He had held the same position as I did. I was surprised and glad to see a familiar face.

The guard went into the reception area to warm himself, so we all had time to talk. I recognized the faces of others in the line whom I had done business with: Yeun Chel Lee, the goods manager of North Ham-Kyung Province; Kim Ung Gil, manager of public security foreign currency; Mr. Kim, fisherman's club assistant; Mr. Jang, director of the Province Central Bank; Kim Soon Ne, gold and silver buyer for the Province Central Bank; Jo Soon Bok, food distribution manager for Chungjin City.

Choi Young Hwan was a close friend of mine. He was originally the assistant manager of the Onsung Province commercial distribution office. In 1982, he was promoted to the commercial managing office where I got to know him well. We had only a short time to talk, but he expressed his concern about me. He said, "Soon Ok, can you survive the torture? You must live so you can tell people the truth about all this. If you die, what will happen to your son and husband? They will misunderstand what has happened and will always say bad things about us."

Right then, the guard came back out into the yard. We stopped talking and sat on our knees in silence.

The moonlight reflected on the snow where it was packed hard from people walking over it. We were sitting in a line on top of the snow as if we were made of stone. Kim Soon Ne, who had been considered an important person in her position at the bank, cried and her shoulders trembled.

The guard, dressed in a warm coat made of dog's hair, walked around us, stamping his booted feet to keep them warm. He mocked us, saying, "Oh, it's so cold. I'm freezing to death." Then he went back into the reception area.

After an hour of sitting on the frigid ground, we all became like frozen fish. When the guard commanded, "Get up!" I could not stand up right away. I fell to the ground many times before I could stand and walk inside.

It was a bit warmer in the pre-interrogation room, so I thought I could get my body thawed out. But we were immediately returned to our prison cells, which weren't much better than being outside. The rooms are very cold and the floors are cement. I placed one of my worn blankets on the floor and used one to cover myself, but the cold from the floor seeped up so that I could not sleep at night. That made sleeping as uncomfortable as an interrogation.

Sometimes the guards would not give me water—not even a single drop—for three or four days. I was so dehydrated that I became uncontrollably dizzy. When I felt the worst, the guards would take me to a table full of food and make me watch people eating. My empty stomach reacted painfully to the sight and smell of food. Right then, they would try to force me to sign the false statement.

In February, Kim Soon Ne from Hwe-Ryung and Cho Soo Bok, who managed the Soo-book grocery store in Chungjin City, were moved into my room, probably because their cells were needed for new prisoners. Since I had been alone in my cell since I arrived, I didn't know much about the interrogation center. I learned more from my cellmates.

During the day, we were interrogated at different times. Although we were not allowed to talk openly, on the nights we did not go to the interrogation office we whispered quietly. To sleep, we put three blankets on the floor and covered ourselves with the other three blankets and hugged each other to keep warm. We listened to and comforted each other and became close friends.

My cellmates told me that most of the people I met in the yard were arrested for refusing to give bribes to their superiors. Since these prisoners were all here because of someone's revenge, they were tortured even more intensely than the real criminals. And this was just the pre-interrogation process. There was more to come.

Chapter 3

DAYS OF TORTURE AND BETRAYAL

EARLY IN MARCH 1987, HAK NAM KIM called me into the interrogation room. He looked at me and said, "This b—— has been here for four months and has not confessed, so we must change her lesson." He hit my ears several times, then dragged me to a room I had not seen before. The room contained a wooden bed that was 2 meters (6 feet) long and 80 centimeters (30 inches) wide. Attached to the bed were three leather belts 60 centimeters (2 feet) long and 20 centimeters (8 inches) wide. In front of the bed on a table sat a big iron water kettle. Immediately sensing that I was going to endure some terrible new torture, my body started to feel pain.

Suddenly, Hak Nam Kim kicked my legs and knocked me onto the wooden bed. He tightly strapped my chest, arms, and legs to the bed. Then he grabbed the water pot and shoved its spout into my mouth. The water filled my mouth then began pumping down into my throat and came out of my nose.

Whenever my torturers hit me with leathers strips or a rubber stick or put pine tree sticks between my fingers and twisted them, I bit my teeth and survived the pain. However, this water torture was worse than any of the other tortures I had endured. I felt darkness falling over me, and it seemed as if my whole body were floating in the air. So much water poured into my body that it felt as if my heart stopped. Then I lost consciousness.

Some time later when I awoke, I saw a wooden board on my stomach. Hak Nam Kim and the section chief pushed down on the board with their black boots. I began to vomit all the water and contents of my stomach until even the bitter stomach acid flowed out. The pain was so bad that I felt as if water were pouring out of every part of my body. Water gushed from my mouth and nose and my bladder. My clothes were soaked.

I heard a dim, sarcastic voice say, "This b——— is not moving at all. Is she dead?" The sound of the voice was like the buzz of little bees.

When they finished, I had gone through so much that I couldn't even stand, so other prisoners dragged me back to my cell. That night, I had a very high fever and began to speak deliriously. My body and face were so swollen that I couldn't even open my eyes. My bladder felt so full that I thought it was going to pop, yet when I tried to urinate, only a few drops of blood mixed with urine came out. For days, I didn't know when the sun came up or when night fell. My cellmates begged the prison guards to give me some medicine, but I don't even remember taking it. They covered my body with all their blankets and slept on the plain cement floor.

Gradually, my temperature went down a little bit, and I regained consciousness. But whenever I tried to get up, my body was so weak that I couldn't even walk. If I had been that sick before when I lived in my house, I probably would have died. But I found out that humans can adjust to any environment. Because of my previous inhumane treatment, I had an almost supernatural power to survive.

After fifteen days, I was able to stand up. My entire body was covered with bruises. Because we had no mirror in our cell, my two friends told me that my skin was as colorful as a snake, blue and black and red.

The skin on my face was very painful, so I touched my lips and felt a long cut across my face. I asked Soon Ne what happened to my face. She said, "When they brought you back from the water torture, your skin had already been sliced and looked very painful."

When I thought about what had happened in that room, I remembered that when the men put the edge of the water kettle to my mouth, I tried to resist. The iron pot had a sharp edge that hit my mouth and must have cut it open.

As the days went by, I felt like I was living in a hell. Everything seemed hopeless, and I was filled with deep sorrow. I was overwhelmed by how badly I was treated. I kept asking myself, *What did I do wrong? How did I hurt the Party or the people? I did not offer bribes to Kim Jung Gung, the security chief of Onsung Province. Is this how I get repaid for my service—with revenge? How could one person make me suffer like this? How could the law allow this?*

Hak Nam Kim kept asking me to sign a statement admitting to embezzling national government property. If I put my signature on a falsified statement, my whole family would no longer receive benefits from the Communist Party. I still refused to sign it. So he kept doing all kinds of painful interrogation to make me sign the false statement.

Toward the end of March, Kim Soon Ne, Cho Soo Bok, and I were forced to make and carry bricks on an iron board. It was very heavy. Because of my weak physical condition, I could not control my body and fell often. The guard would kick me fiercely and continuously with his shoe.

I Regret That I Said Too Much

Some time before April 15, which is Kim Il Sung's birthday and a national holiday, the province security bureau received an inquiry about the ten prisoners who used to work for the Party. The officials received orders to close the cases as quickly as possible and release the prisoners by April 15. This order came from the central government.

On April 13, I was not called out until late morning. Hak Nam Kim entered my cell and said, "Today, the political section comrade and the inspection section chief comrade are coming down to the assembly place to meet you. Don't say anything to them. Just confess your crimes. Are you going to do it or not?" Then he left.

A little later, a guard took me to the office manager's room. On the way, the guard said, "This is the first time in the seven years I have worked here that the political section chief has come here. Maybe it's because the Communist Party wants some of the prisoners to be released."

When I entered the room, I saw two high-level officers, a colonel who was very fat and a political section officer who was tall and skinny. They looked about in their mid-fifties. I bowed slightly.

They looked me over. I was just bones. I had no skin or fat. *I look very ugly*, I thought.

They didn't say anything for quite a while, just looked at me from top to bottom. Although my clothes covered most of my body, the exposed areas looked very bad. I had bruises everywhere. My ears had frostbite and were swollen like an animal's ears. My face was black and blue and my mouth still had not healed where I got hurt during the water torture. My frostbitten feet were swollen and pus drained out. In fact, I was barefoot because my feet were so huge that I couldn't even wear shoes.

The two officers came closer to me. One asked me, "Why does your face look like that?"

I did not answer.

Then he asked, "Why are your feet so swollen? Why aren't you wear-ing shoes?" He kept asking me questions I could not answer because I was not sure why they had come to see me. If I said the wrong things, I might be tortured again.

The political section chief said, "Pull up your trouser leg."

I pulled up a little bit of my pant leg. My leg was swollen and bruised. It didn't even look like the flesh of a human being.

The two of them also inspected my body. My bruises were so bad that they couldn't stand to look at them for long.

The inspection chief said, "Why did you do nothing when they beat you like this?"

I couldn't believe he asked me this. How could a person under their control even resist? Even a three-year-old would understand that. *He must be joking,* I thought.

Then he asked me, "What were you thinking while you were being interrogated for the last few months? If you tell the truth, I'll send you home. Although I am wearing a uniform, I came on behalf of the Com-munist Party, so tell me your true feelings."

I thought that because he was the security bureau political section chief, he must also be a member of the Party, so I began telling all I had inside me. First I said, "I am a Communist Party member and I have not done anything wrong. They brought me here without telling me where I was to be sent. They kidnapped me while I was working in my office and have insisted that I acknowledge something that I have not done." I described in detail what they had done to me.

As the tall political section chief looked over his eyeglasses at me, I implored, "Please bring out the truth. I cannot die in here without the truth being told. If I die without the truth ever being discovered about me, my husband and son will hate me."

The section chief listened carefully without speaking.

I continued, "One thing I am sure of, I have not embezzled any of the national property nor have I offered anyone a bribe. I performed my responsibility; I worked hard for many, many years. The Onsung County bureau chief kept asking me, 'Did you offer bribes to any officers of the Party?' They brought up the name of Park Kwang Sam, Party secretary of the country, to undermine him. They wanted to find out if I had received anything from Park Kwang Sam or if I had given him anything. By law, the security bureau cannot investigate Party officers, so I don't know why this has been done to me."

I insisted, "According to Kim Il Sung's decrees, the executive department of the government can't investigate the Communist Party." Then I explained what was happening within the farmer's assembly places. "The prison officers take away the food allocated to the prisoners and exchange it for liquor. They give the prisoners food that only animals should eat. This is happening not only to me, but also to twelve other innocent people. We have not done anything wrong and did not steal anything, nor did we commit conspiracy. This is totally unreasonable. We have given our best allegiance to the Party, and we don't understand this situation."

As I talked, the two officers didn't move a muscle in their faces. I poured out everything in my heart like a waterfall on a mountain. I didn't know that these two had come to trick me and find out what I was thinking. They made me believe that they were party members. They lied to me to find out what I would tell about my position. I described it very vividly and strongly.

All for Their Own Greed

To outsiders, the North Korean government looks unified like metal pieces seamlessly welded together, but in reality, the Party and the security bureau officials all work to satisfy their own greed and to fill their own fat stomachs. The political chief, who said he was a Party member, wanted to support his own people and push me into a corner.

The trouble all began in October 1986, right before I was arrested. A big social issue surfaced concerning officials abusing human rights, which caused the central party government to inspect the executive branch. What was going on was that the people in the provincial offices began to ask special favors of the ordinary workers in the commerce department. If the workers refused to give what was demanded, they were sent to concentration camps out of revenge. As many commerce department workers were arrested on false charges, the central government began to inspect the security police. The police were then afraid of getting caught by the government, so they framed the chairmen of the commerce departments to hide what they did wrong.

The executive branch authorities victimized the commerce department chairmen that they did not like. They falsely accused them of embezzling goods that the officials themselves had received. That is why the agents desperately wanted me to sign the paper. They had to find someone to take the fall for their crimes. As the problem continued, the conflict between the police officers and the Communist Party grew worse. The more the government tried to solve the problem, the more people like me became victims.

In my situation, the Onsung security bureau had already inspected and found no real evidence of wrongdoing. That is why they tortured me so severely to get me to sign a false statement. If I were released, I would cause them more problems. The security bureau officials knew I would go to the Party and request a hearing, which would put the bureau chief in a difficult position.

What made my situation worse was that Kim Mun So and his family of eleven had stolen a ship that belonged to the Public Security Bureau (PSB) and escaped from North Korea to Japan. That made the PSB look bad. Now if the Communist Party found out that the province security inspection department chief was responsible for my arrest, he would be removed.

The security bureau officials must have decided that if they released me, I would talk and they would be interrogated for my wrongful arrest. I fell into their trap and could not get out of it. Even today, I regret all the things I said and did that day.

Therefore, Hak Nam Kim acted like an animal with a very hot temper as he continued the torture. As time had passed, the beatings had slowed a bit, but now every night I was brought to the interrogation room and asked the same questions over and over. He kept insisting that I sign the statement. He shouted, "Once you were in a position where you controlled everything because you were part of the Communist Party. Now you are in our hands. If you don't want to die early, sign the statement. The longer you wait, the more likely you will become a ghost." As he shouted, he twisted my fingers.

Then Hak Nam Kim changed his torturing method and gave me less and less food. Because of malnutrition and the frozen fish torture that winter, the frostbite on my feet and ears swelled even more and became red with infection. I had so much pain that I couldn't sleep at night. I was so dizzy that one or two blows would make me fall. If I fell during the torture, they would drag me like a dead animal to the water pot and pour cold water all over my body. Sometimes they brought me back to the prison cell with wet clothes. Because I did not have a change of clothing, I had to try to sleep in my cold, wet clothes.

So Many Victims

I personally knew some victims who were in the same position as I was. Yun Chel Lee was manager of the North Ham-Kyung Province. Because he refused to give televisions to police officers, he was arrested and tortured in revenge. He was a very well-educated, trusted worker. He had a good reputation for making successful trades of North Korean foods, such as mushrooms, mackerel eggs, and rare vegetables, in exchange for Japanese electric appliances, refrigerators, color televisions, VCRs, and men's suits. He also imported goods for the relatives of Kim Il Sung. Since he had control over special and valuable goods, all high government officials made demands on him. He usually granted their requests. However, when the police officers kept asking for televisions, Yun Chel Lee had to refuse because TVs were not easy to sneak out.

He was arrested and taken to the interrogation center seven days before I was arrested. His arrest happened unexpectedly while he was working at his office in his suit and dress shoes. I met him in April 1987 when the guards changed their policy toward us twelve political prisoners. At that time, they began allowing us to have a one-hour exercise period and to do laundry. This happened because all the inspectors returned to the province security department and the guards took over their jobs.

Yun Chel Lee was a gentleman. When he saw me, he burst into tears. I forgot my own condition as I looked at him. His body had bruises all over it. He could not use his right leg and had to pull it along.

During that January when the guards took us out for the frozen fish torture, Yun Chel Lee's ears had gotten frostbitten and swelled to the size of a child's hand. Yellow pus ran down under his chin. It looked so gross. Because of his terrible torture, Yun Chel Lee had become half paralyzed. When he tried to stand, he couldn't control his body and he just fell over. He could not eat much. Within a few months, the man I had known who had a passion for business and never told a lie totally disappeared. He had become less than human.

Choi Young Hwan of Hwe-Ryung County's commercial managing department received even greater torture. When I knew him, he was fifty-four years old and as a young man had served in the Korean War in the Nag-dong River conflict. Because he was wounded, he had retired as an honorary veteran.

He ended up in the middle of the power struggle between the department of inspection and the security bureau. When he managed the commerce department, all the officers roomed together. Every time they asked, he tried to provide as much as they desired. But the public prosecutor felt he was not receiving as much as the public security bureau inspector. He asked for a big item, a color television, although he knew that Choi Young Hwan could not easily get a television out.

Reluctantly, Choi Young Hwan secretly gave a television to the public prosecutor. But the Party later found out. He confessed the name of the public prosecutor, who then had to return the television. The public prosecutor was angry at Choi Young Hwan and soon had him arrested.

When Choi Young Hwan came to the center, they interrogated him to find out who he sold products to and what kinds of bribes he took. He was tortured every day. When he was pushed into the brick furnace, his hands touched the walls and his palms were severely burned. He did not get medical treatment and after three months his burns still had not healed.

Sometimes he poured his salty soup over his hands as a disinfectant. But because he was so hungry, he then ate the soup he had poured over his hands with the pus in it. As the burns got worse, the pus mixed with blood from his hands infected his whole body. He became paralyzed from the waist down and did not know when he urinated or had a bowel movement. Because of his smell, the guards treated him badly and the people around him gave him very bad looks.

When he urinated on himself or had a bowel movement, other prisoners dragged him outside into the yard and poured cold water over him. He didn't feel cold or hot sensation because he was getting old and his body had been weakened by the torture.

Toward the end of April, he could not survive any more of the severe torture and he left this world. He had three sons and two daughters. I heard later from the hospital doctors that two of his sons were forced out of the army and the third one had to leave school. The whole family was kicked out of Huh Yung City and sent to a farm commune. All their assets and property were confiscated and nothing was given to their children.

When I first met Choi Young Hwan, he said, "If you die here, no one will ever tell the real truth about you, so you must live and the Party will provide answers." He died with his eyes open.

Kim Woong Kil was another innocent victim. As manager of the export department in North Ham-Kyung Province, he sold mackerel eggs, a delicacy. He went out of the country to procure televisions and refrigerators for the province security bureau officials.

Because of his high army ranking, he received greater tortures. He sometimes yelled and resisted until the whole center heard him. He received such severe torture that one of his ears was cut off and the lower part of his body became paralyzed. He later died in the prisoner interrogation room.

One man who worked in the fisherman's club was sixty years old and was tortured every day for something he did not do. He made up a ridiculous confession in which he said that he had sold a whole train from the Chungjin railroad station. Everyone laughed. How could this old man steal a big train, and who would buy it? Later, people called him the railroad engineer. He also lost one ear because of the torture and the other ear was twisted out of shape.

A principal of a woman's junior high school was in the interrogation center for two years. He was suspected of murdering two female teachers. His tragedy began one peaceful morning when he arrived early at school and discovered the two dead teachers lying in a room. As soon as he saw them, he called the police. The police could not find the murderer, so they concluded that the principal was the murderer and had sexually abused the women.

During his years at the interrogation center, he insisted that he did not kill anyone, so they tortured him greatly. In the electric torture, they melted down his two ear lobes until he had only ear holes. All his fingers were melted down and one leg was shortened so he couldn't walk right. His mouth was so twisted that you could hardly distinguish what he was saying. During the two years of his interrogation, his whole body was shortened and he looked like a ten-year-old.

After two years, the police found the real murderers. They had sneaked into the school to steal an accordion. When they saw the two teachers alone, they tried to rape them, then killed them. The murderers were later arrested for stealing, and during their interrogation confessed to the murder of the teachers.

The old principal was released. However, he had become a scary looking, lame man. Although he was proven innocent, no one from the police station or interrogation center ever apologized to him. Instead, they threatened him into signing a paper stating that he would never tell anyone how he was treated at the interrogation center. After his release, he was unable to function in society. He could not eat and the government did not provide any medical treatment for him. His body deteriorated, and he died.

A young man named Kim Kwang Seuk was also sent to the interrogation center. His mother came to North Korea from Japan with him and his twin brother. The twin brother grew up tall and strong. One winter day, they went to the Tumen River at the Chinese border where they met some Chinese people. Their meetings became a problem since the North Korean government does not allow any kind of interaction with foreigners.

Right before they were put into the interrogation center, Kim Kwang Seuk's brother drank poison to commit suicide because he didn't think he would ever get out of the interrogation center. He was hospitalized and underwent surgery. When he recovered from the surgery, he escaped to China. Kim Kwang Seuk stayed in North Korea and was arrested.

All these people were victims. The prisoners all knew that if they did not survive the torture, they would never return to tell the truth. They would die like worthless wild animals. That's what kept some of them alive.

Chapter 4

FOR MY HUSBAND AND SON

ON MAY 19, 1987, SEVEN MONTHS AFTER I was imprisoned, I was moved to the province interrogation center. At this point, I lost my right of citizenship in North Korea. I was also expelled from the Party. This meant that I lost all my rights as a human being. My wish and dream of appealing to a court sometime in the future also disappeared. I gave up hope that the province interrogation center would give me a fair trial or that the Party would help me get back home. The Province Security Bureau had represented my case before the Party with falsified documents. When I heard that the Party planned to turn the case over to the court system, I gave up even the slightest hope that I would be excused for my mischief and sent home.

Hak Nam Kim sent me to another interrogator, Chun Ho Kim, who had a mean-looking horse face. He was as evil as Hak Nam Kim. Once he took over the case, he tortured me night and day to make me sign the falsified statement that Hak Nam Kim had prepared. Because of Chun Ho Kim's repetitive questioning and yelling and the lack of sleep, I was in great pain and my nervous system began to break down.

Since I kept silent all day long, Chun Ho Kim ordered the guard to chain me with fetters to iron bars on the door. He was testing which would last longer: my resistance or his torture. The pain of my body weight held up by the fetters sapped my wrists and ankles. After they released me from the fetters, I could not stand or walk straight because of my weakened condition, and I lost consciousness from time to time.

Once as I regained consciousness, my back itched. I could barely reach my back to scratch. As I did, I caught sight of something crawling. Through swollen eyes, I saw maggots all over my back. Flies had landed on my deadened flesh and laid their eggs as I was unconscious for hours.

Chun Ho Kim constantly threatened me, "You b——, I've been working in this job for twenty years. To me, killing a person is as easy as eating cool soup. Don't even think about getting out of this place alive unless you agree that what is black is white." His furor to get me to sign the false statement was so great that he jumped up and down like a tiger with a burned back. Yet I resisted, placing my life as collateral for the truth. I told him, "I will never admit to a crime I have not committed."

Chun Ho Kim sent many police officers to interrogate me, and their responsibility was to convince me to sign. One said, "You know what? If we release you, the police chief who sent you here will be fired. Think about who I prefer to help, you or the police chief."

That night I returned to my cell by putting one hand on the wall to help me walk, and I fell many times. A jailer came by and kicked me, saying, "Yeh! Don't fake it. If you don't want to be chained to the iron bars again, get up and walk!"

When I could not get up, the guards pulled my arm and dragged me like a dead dog into my cell, cursing as they went. One jailer said as he turned away, "She is paying for despising lower level people like us when she lived outside the prison. But now she is tasting our strong hand of torture." Even guards who knew nothing about my case treated me like a criminal.

The cold weather was as cruel as the jailers. The building had no heat in the winter. Worse yet, the interrogator ordered, "We have to freeze her to make her feel miserable so that she cannot tolerate any more, and then she will confess her crimes." He opened my window so that cold wind and snowflakes blew into my cell and froze my body. It was too cold to sleep.

The Plight of the Prisoners

I soon found that in the province interrogation center, two groups of twelve jailers worked in shifts. Even though most of them were lower ranking officers in their twenties, they were proud of their position so

That night snowflakes blew into my cell and froze my body.

they treated the prisoners brutally. They abused prisoners who came from other concentration centers more harshly because these were people the other centers had given up on. The prison had twenty cells, ten on each side of a long hallway with a walkway in between. Each cell had a back door about the size of a dog. Prisoners had to crawl through the door to enter or exit the cell. Because of the walls between each cell, prisoners didn't know who was in the next cell. But if you stayed long enough, you could guess your neighbor's name and home town by listening to the jailers.

When prisoners were not taken to the interrogation room, they were forced to sit in the jail cell with crossed legs and head bowed. They were not allowed to move even a fingertip. This immobility lasted from 5 a.m. until 10 p.m. After remaining motionless for seventeen hours, our hips and legs became numb and swollen. This was a very difficult torture to endure.

Two jailers walked back and forth in front of the cells, watching for any movement. If a jailer saw a prisoner move, he commanded the person to stand and yelled, "Yah! You b———. Why did you move? Does your body tickle because I am not hitting you? Stick your hands out between the iron bars."

Once the prisoners stuck out their hands, the jailer smacked the top of their fingers with a rubber club. As they struck the fingers, the jailers yelled, "Spread out your fingers." If the prisoners did not obey, the jailer hit them ten more times. After the beating, the prisoners' hands became swollen and they could not move their fingers for a long time. If the prisoners hesitated to stick out their hands, the jailers stabbed the prisoner's body with a long wooden stick.

After sitting motionless for hours, the prisoners looked forward to the arrival of the trash collectors so they could stretch their legs a bit, although the time was short. The prisoners waited for their turn to hand the toilet paper through the back door.

Sometimes the cleaning guard looked for a volunteer by yelling, "Is there anyone who has not done anything wrong today? Is there someone who's strong enough to do this work?" Invariably, someone would come forward just to have a moment of release.

One time, a crazy prisoner called out, "Your honor, allow me to do that work." Then guard Young Ho Kim screamed, "Who said that? Stand up!"

Kim made that prisoner stand in front of the iron-bar cell door. He started to poke his body with a pointed bamboo stick while he screamed, "S.O.B., who allowed you to speak? I will kill you." He continued to poke the prisoner severely.

After I was imprisoned in the province interrogation center, I was given only a crust of dried corn with a few beans in it to eat. The food was supposed to have 30 percent beans and 70 percent corn, however, the jailers took most of the beans to eat themselves. Then the jailers threatened the prisoners, "Don't you ever tell anyone that you did not get your beans! The day you tell someone, we will break your ribs!"

One day, a man who had worked as a manager on a farm told his interrogator that he did not have any beans with his rice. After that, the jailers did not allow him to sleep. They made him stand on his feet all night. If he became drowsy or began to sway, a jailer jabbed him with a long wooden stick. Two days later, he wailed and begged the jailer for forgiveness.

After that incident, I saw about ten jailers sharing a big bowl of beans. As they were eating the ration of beans intended for the prisoners, they did not even cover their disgusting behavior. They threatened the prisoners, "If you let out a word about this, we will rip your mouth off. You had fat bellies from the good food you had before you came to prison."

A worse torture than beating was when a guard brought a fish from the cafeteria and broiled it on the hallway coal stove. The smell of cooking fish turned the prisoners' stomachs upside down. While the guards ate the fish, they would taunt, "You dogs, I know you want to eat, but I let this smell bring more appetite to your mouth. What fun to see your faces changing like that!"

Each of the twenty-four guards had his own evil way of dealing with prisoners. Some of the jailers didn't have reason to beat the prisoners, so they just cursed at them and made them stand all day long. It seemed to me as if they enjoyed seeing the pain in the prisoners' faces. They were very clever at knowing how to drive the prisoners crazy. Some jailers treated them like toys. Sometimes they called out their "damaged toys" and kicked and hit them as if they were practicing their military arts. They abused the prisoners until they lost consciousness.

When Young Ho Kim came to guard during the cold winter, he wore a long, dog-skin jacket. He opened all the windows of the prison building all day and night. As he opened the windows, he complained, "Pew! These stinking things! They make it awfully hard to breathe!" The cold wind froze fingers and toes and the prisoners had frostbite all over their bodies.

Another jailer closed all the windows and filled the jail with smoke from the coal stove to make the prisoners sneeze. If a prisoner sneezed, the jailer would beat him.

I noticed that males were more easily affected by the inhumane treatment than females. In the province interrogation center, men turned into living skeletons within three months. Their heads were shaved and their skin looked like it was glued to the surface of their bones. Woong Kil Kim, the manager of the export department, was transferred to the province interrogation center. Soon after he arrived, he died.

The Promise

Chun Ho Kim kept torturing me furiously. Miraculously, my fatigued body and mind endured every minute. Finally, Chun Ho Kim ran out of patience. He screamed, "This stupid, forgetful thing! When I beat you, you promise me you will sign the statement; but when I stop beating, you forget what you just said!"

Chun Ho Kim, however, was not a simple-minded person. When he realized that torture would never make me sign, he changed his strategy to appeasement. He sympathetically said, "Remember last year? You persisted, but you have nothing left but scars. Why don't you just sign here? If you sign, I promise that I will make sure your son and husband can stay where they are right now. If you keep up your stubborn act, you and your entire family will be destroyed. Which would be more beneficial?"

I pondered all night about what he had told me. I thought, *They'll never release me. And if I do not sign, I will eventually die from all the torture. Then people will never know the truth, and my son and husband will be dragged to a rural town as forced laborers. On the other hand, Chun Ho Kim promised me if I sign, he will save my family.*

The next morning, I finally decided to sign the written statement. Chun Ho Kim said gleefully, "Now you've finally yielded to me. I told you I can make everything turn out the way I want. I could even get you to say black is white when it is really black. I always win because I'm the one holding the knife."

I saw his smile of satisfaction, but my mind was filled with darkness. Although I had withstood the torture to keep the truth for a whole year, everything had become so meaningless. At the end of October 1987, my trembling hand signed the written statement without considering what was coming next.

The PSB told me that my public trial was set for November 19 in my hometown in Onsung County. I had a little hope that I might be able to proclaim my innocence at the trial. I wanted to at least tell the truth to my husband and to the Party. I even had hopes that I would see my husband. With that mindset, I waited for the day of my public trial.

Finally the day came to leave for my home and work place. Before I left, Chun Ho Kim warned me, "Don't you dare say anything in the public trial other than what you promised me. Remember, the future of your family depends on your behavior." However, I was convinced that I would be able to tell my husband the truth.

On the day before my trial, I arrived at Onsung station at 3 p.m. It was a cold day. My eyes caught sight of my house, but I couldn't go to the door and meet my husband. Suddenly, I was flooded with emotion and tears poured down like rain.

A police car was waiting in front of Onsung Station to transfer me to jail. When I arrived at the police station, I saw all the familiar police officers I had once known. I noticed their astonished faces when they saw my bruised body. The police officer who had worked the hardest to ruin my life could not hide his startled face either. Since he had been under government suspicion, he was now anxious to make sure people thought I was guilty. That's why he had planned the public trial. He was afraid I would tell people the truth, so he commanded that I be put into solitary confinement. Here I was back in my hometown, but I was still alone. No one came to talk to me; everyone totally ignored me.

Although my body was exhausted from the seven-hour train ride, my mind was clear. I thought, *Until last year, I was free and faithful to Kim Il Sung and to the government. So what brought me here? What did I do that was so wrong to deserve all this?* I could not find an answer to my questions. I changed my line of thinking: *I am sure my husband will come to see me tomorrow. Probably my son can't come because he is in college in Pyongyang. I wonder if he knows about what has happened to me.* My heart overflowed with my desire to see my husband and son.

My train of thought was interrupted when I heard steps coming from a short distance. I recognized the face of one of my husband's students. I was so glad to see someone I knew!

I skipped right over the greeting and abruptly asked him, "Your name is Chel Ho, right? How is my husband doing?"

He hesitated. "Please don't misunderstand. I am not allowed to talk to you. The police chief said that whoever converses with you will be punished."

I was stunned by the police chief's threats. At the same time, I felt awkward listening to such a polite voice since I was used to hearing all kinds of curse words at the interrogation center. I wanted to beg him to tell me about my family, but I didn't because I was afraid of getting him into trouble.

The Trial

Daybreak came. I was led into an auditorium for my public trial. People filled the room and overflowed to the outside. I learned later that the police chief had publicized that I had embezzled a huge amount of public funds. He also said that the government's economy was deteriorating because of people like me. That was the PSB's way of shifting the blame of hard economic conditions to a few innocent people. Curious, about a thousand people in my hometown gathered to see their old neighbor's trial.

I asked to see my husband before the trial began. At that time, I didn't know anything about the law. I figured that before a trial started, a judge and an attorney would meet the accused person and listen to him. Since no one ever came and said, "I'm your judge or attorney," I figured I would have to stand alone in the courtroom. I felt that having my husband there would make me strong. My greatest desire was to meet my husband and tell him the truth. Before I entered the courtroom, I begged a jailer to let me see my husband.

He answered, "Shut up! Your husband did not come. Don't try to see anybody. By the way, don't say anything other than what you promised us."

I could not believe that my husband did not come to see me. Then I realized that my husband was my only witness; that's why the police chief didn't let him come. The only reason the police put me on trial was to deceive people into thinking I was guilty.

The pre-trial began at 10 a.m. at the Commerce office where I had worked for seventeen years. The names of the judge, public prosecutor, attorney, and two juries were announced. After judge Kim Moon Kyu stated the case, the public prosecutor asked me whether I admitted my crime. When I heard him say that, anger exploded in my heart. I protested, "No, it is not true! I never embezzled public funds. I did not do anything to deserve this. Please, see the truth."

The two jailers who sat on either side of me kicked my legs and said, "Are you crazy?" The judge then concluded the first part of the trial. This all took place in fifteen minutes. I hobbled out with sore legs and a restless mind.

I was led into an auditorium for the public trial.

They put me back in jail to wait for the next part of the trial, set for 5 p.m. A police officer came into my jail cell and threatened, "If you cause problems in court, you will pay for it. Wise up! You do not want to ruin the lives of your husband and son, do you? If you just say 'yes' in court, at least your family will be safe. It is best for them that you finish this case smoothly, and you will go quietly to prison. You have a choice. One is to do what I told you. The other is to be rebellious and then be secretly killed by us. If you die, I will cancel the trial, and you will be listed as a missing prisoner."

Finally, the time for the trial arrived. The public prosecutor asked me once again, "Do you admit your crime?"

I quietly answered, "Yes, I broke the trust of the government."

The judge skipped the rest of the trial procedure and sentenced me to thirteen years at the resocialization prison for embezzling public funds. Throughout the whole trial, my attorney did not say a word to defend me. He came only to formally occupy a seat. No one told my son or husband about the trial. I did not even have a witness to speak up for me.

Until I was sentenced, I continued to believe in Kim Il Sung and the Party. All that happened to me was just because middle ranking officers took revenge when they did not receive what they wanted. I believed that if the Party knew what was happening to me, they would not let this happen. Then in court, I had to say that I did not continually, faithfully provide my utmost to Kim Il Sung's political trust. That was a severe crime. That is why I fought for an entire year to avoid admitting to something I did not do.

To the Prisoner Transfer Center

After the trial, I boarded a train for Chungjin City. The workers from the commercial department came to see me off. They sympathized with me by saying, "What happened to you could happen to us at any time." Their tear-streaked faces followed me to the station and warmly encouraged me, "You must survive. We will see you later."

As the train began to move, I was heartbroken about leaving my hometown without hearing about my family. I didn't know when I would ever see them again. I worried about my family and their shock when they heard about my heavy sentence. However, I was so glad I could keep my husband and son safe. I believed the interrogators' promise that they would not do anything to harm my family.

I comforted myself by thinking, *My husband can support my son's college expenses. I will be in prison, but I will be happy to hear about my son's success. At least the court didn't confiscate my family's property so my husband and son will not have problems supporting themselves.*

A guard appeared in my compartment carrying a pack. He said, "I guess your employees still like you. The sales clerk, Young Hee, brought you lunch."

He opened the pack. Inside were two bottles of liquor, five boxes of cigarettes, two packs of candy, rice, and rice cakes. Young Hee knew that I liked rice cakes, so she had specially prepared them for me. When I had climbed onto the train, I had seen her face from a distance. My tears had blurred my vision, so I couldn't see her clearly. Through her tears, she had waved at me. She boarded the train to tell me about my family, but the guards would not allow her to see me. She offered liquor and cigarettes to them if they would give their permission. She begged for a couple of minutes, but they firmly refused her request. The guards told her that they would get fired if they let anyone talk to me. Finally, Young Hee gave up trying to see me. After sending me lunch, she got off at the next stop.

The guards devoured all the food that Young Hee had brought for me. They did not even offer me a bite. They rudely said, "It's like a birthday meal. We have not had rice cakes since last year." The court prosecutor, who rode with the guards, asked for some rice. One court worker hid a pack of candy in his pocket. Later, a guard looked for the candy, but the court worker pretended not to know anything. They soon finished the food and then shared the cigarettes. Furious, I cursed them silently. *You shameless swindlers! Eat and die from an overstuffed stomach!*

After arriving at Sunchen station, I was taken to the prisoner transfer center. Three days after my trial, I received a written judgment to sign. I couldn't accept the thirteen-year sentence. I thought, *The people who sentenced me to thirteen years don't have enough integrity to decide my life. They are the kind of people who snatch a starving prisoner's lunch and hide candy.*

The written judgment said that a prisoner who did not agree with his sentence could appeal to a higher court within ten days. I decided to appeal instead of signing the written judgment. An interrogator who heard about my decision threatened me. "You chose to have the trial, now you should be satisfied with the result. You may think you could get a lighter sentence by appealing to the higher court, but what will really happen is that your case will go back to the same judge. And he may extend your sentence from thirteen years to twenty years. Think carefully before you decide."

After the interrogator left, I began to question my decision to appeal. I didn't trust North Korean judges, and I knew that they could extend my sentence if they wanted to.

The next morning, a jailer said to me, "I tell you what! I've been working here for seven years, but I have never seen one person get a lighter sentence by appealing to a higher court. Let me give you a piece of advice. If you do not want to die here, you'd better leave as soon as possible. Also, if you go to the prison, you will have a better chance to appeal to a higher court."

After listening to him, I decided to appeal once I got to prison.

The Place Where What Is False Becomes Truth

At the prison transfer center, people could be killed without a trial. Therefore, the center had many executions. Prisoners who had not had a public trial were executed at night and then buried in the mountains.

The center had a special torture room where prisoners could be frozen or baked. This torture was performed between 1 and 2 a.m. The torture room was about 60 centimeters (2 feet) wide and had an adjustable ceiling. There was only room for a person to sit on the floor and put his head between his knees. Jailers called this room the place where what is false becomes truth. A jailer once threatened me, "If you do not want to be a frozen fish, you'd better do what we tell you to do."

In October 1987, a seventeen-year-old boy, the son of an iron mill worker, was dragged into the prisoner transfer center. He was accused of being the leader of a gang fight. Gangs were strictly prohibited in North Korea because they could develop into anti-government terrorist groups. One night, this young boy was pulled out of the torture room, frozen to death.

A man from the north side of Chungjin City went insane because of continuous torture and lack of sleep. He insulted Kim Il Sung by saying, "What did Kim Il Sung do for me?" In North Korea, whoever insults or complains about Kim Il Sung is killed instantly. A jailer froze this insane man to death.

Another common kind of torture room is an iron closet. People are confined in the closet and hit by a club that has countless sharp nails sticking out of it. Any prisoner who offended the jailers or interrogators was beaten by this thorn club. One slight hit made a person bleed. Prisoners who were beaten with the thorn club became very sinister looking from the scars all over their body.

I shared a cell with a young lady named Mee Sook Kim. She was twenty-one years old, very pretty and nice. She was arrested because she helped her boss give away corn to coal miners. Although she might be released, her life will be ruined because people will always think of her as a criminal.

She was raped by her interrogator. He appeased her by promising that if she would keep his crime secret, he would set her free. To complete her misery, she became pregnant. The interrogator took her to a hospital where the baby was aborted.

The interrogator worried that if she and I shared the same cell for long, I might spread rumors about what he had done to Mee Sook Kim, so he pressured the authorities to send me to a prison. Just for that, I was sent into an unknown pitfall.

Chapter 5

To the Den of the Tailless Animals

ON NOVEMBER 23, 1987, AT 9 A.M., my train arrived at Khechen Station. That was the day I was imprisoned in the resocialization center located in Khechen City in South Pyong-An Province. This prison was a place where more than actual criminals were taken. Citizens who were accused of not obeying the rules of the government were also sent there.

Weak in mind and body, I stepped out of the train into a cold winter day. The gloomy sky spread snowflakes in the air. My attention was captivated by people in the station since I had not been outside a prison for a long time. I saw young students walking fast and women carrying heavy baggage on their heads.

In front of the station cafeteria, I saw an old man wearing a worn-out shirt and pants. The shivering, starving old man begged for food and money by bowing to people. His ragged appearance surprised me because until then I had never thought that there were poor people in North Korea. I thought those conditions existed only during the years of Japanese colonial occupation in Korea.

The sights shocked me into a trance until the guards urged me to snap out of it. People getting off the train glanced at my bruised body. I knew they thought I was a desperate criminal.

When I had left the prisoner transfer center, I had told myself, *I am not a criminal. I did nothing to deserve this. I am just a victim of someone's revenge. At some time I will proclaim the truth and regain my citizenship and my membership in the Party.*

Yet in spite of my determination not to consider myself a criminal, I already felt intimidated. I followed the guards into a station cafeteria that had about ten small tables. One guard paid for three slices of corn bread and a bowl of cabbage soup. That was the first time I had seen real food in fourteen months.

The guard pushed the food toward me. "This may be the last good meal you will eat in your life. I am not supposed to buy you this, but since I know all about your circumstances and your friend in Onsung gave me the money, I am buying this for your last meal."

After more than twenty hours of train travel in which I was constantly humiliated by people staring at me, I had no appetite. Two guards took out their rice balls from their packs and devoured them. While I watched them eat, a filthy hand from behind my back snatched my corn bread. I turned to see a ten-year-old boy cram the bread into his mouth. My heart ached as I witnessed this sad reality. I laid my head on the table and thought, *This is not the world I knew.*

The guard grabbed the little boy, then hit him and threatened him. The boy's shoulders trembled with fear. I stood up and begged the guard to release him. "I'm not hungry, so please send the rest of my bread with him. This is the last request I make before I go to prison."

The guard released the boy as he bluntly answered, "It's your decision. It was your bread."

I stared at the skinny, haggard boy and placed the rest of the bread into his dirty hands. I followed the guards out of the cafeteria. This seemed like such a nightmare.

When I passed the Khechen Department Store, I remembered the time I attended the commercial training program in the store. How excited I was then to be a worker for the government. After the training, I called together all my coworkers and explained how to apply what I had learned. Now, years later, I was walking by as a dejected prisoner. As I looked up at the big sign on the store, the letters of the sign seemed to come alive. They said, "Hey! Here is the manager of the commercial department. She is a prisoner now. What did she do to end up in prison? She looks so pathetic."

A filthy hand from behind my back snatched my corn bread.

While I was in the interrogation center, I had missed the real world. I had thought I would enjoy watching people while I was being transferred to the prison. But the people's lives were so hard; I felt unhappy when I observed their hardships. I could barely open my eyes because snowflakes constantly hit my face.

One guard sarcastically commented, "Today's weather matches her mood."

Number 832

I quietly followed the guards who were walking very fast. They wanted to get me quickly to the prison so they could go home. They kept urging me to walk faster.

Finally, the darkly painted prison appeared in the corner of the valley. The closer we got, the more scared I felt. As we walked, a crow sitting on a light pole cawed loudly. The crow is a symbol of bad luck, and it was the first thing to greet me in the prison valley!

One guard made a strange remark, "Do you know what the crow is saying to you? It is saying, 'Are you going to prison? If you do, goodbye. I will see you later.'"

I smiled bitterly.

As we turned into the corner of the valley, I was overwhelmed by the sight of the monstrous prison complex surrounded by two fences: a huge concrete fence 10 meters (33 feet) high and high-voltage barbed wire. Soldiers guarded the prison in six different places.

I felt like I was suffocating. I thought, *I can't get any closer to the building.* I stopped and tried to run away, but I was carried into the prison by the two guards. I passed through a metal prison door and entered a registration office where a lieutenant was waiting for us. He glanced at me and took a document from the guards. That was the simple transfer procedure.

The first thing the lieutenant told me was a brutal glimpse of my new reality. "You are not a human being anymore. If you want to survive here, you'd better give up the idea that you are human." He assigned me the number 832. That was how my thirteen-year sentence began. The painful months of my interrogation were only a prelude to my misery. I was now considered less than human—a tailless animal.

Chapter 6

Hard Labor, Cold, and Starvation

THE RESOCIALIZATION PRISON HAD TWO buildings. One was two stories and the other was three. The top floor of the three-story building had a kitchen, bathroom, and laundry room. The second floor held an auditorium with a high ceiling and was designed for orienting new prisoners. Except for the walls, everything in the prison was painted black. This made me afraid of what was ahead of me in my prison life.

The prison complex also had a large factory that was about 150 meters (500 feet) away from the prison. It was a two-story, square building separated into two parts: male prisoners worked on one side and female prisoners on the other.

The reception guard handed me over to a cell control guard who commanded me to sit on my knees in the hallway. He held a document containing my statistics, and he began to confirm my name, age, previous job, and the crime I had committed.

When he asked about my crime, I answered, "I am unjustly accused. Everything was the scheme of the security bureau chief. I am begging for your help in appealing to a higher court while I am here in prison."

Until that moment, I really believed what the jailer in the prison transfer center had told me—that I would have a chance to appeal to a higher court while I was in prison. Now as I demanded justice, a fifty-five-year-old female prison officer kicked me in the chest. I was not prepared for her blow, so I fell over. As I fell, I heard her say with a strong northern Korean accent, "You want justice, huh? What do you mean you were not treated justly? You must not know what kind of place this is. You have lots of lessons to learn!" She kicked me again and added, "You must give up being human if you want to survive here. That is the only way to survive."

Deep despair and confusion came over me like the sound of the iron prison gate closing. I couldn't understand how a person could consider another person as not even human.

Newcomer's Cell

A cell control guard called for utility workers and two female prisoners quickly came forward. They sat on their knees with their heads bowed. "Sir, we are here as you called," they said. Their actions and speech seemed bizarre. The guard ordered them to take me to the bathroom to change my clothes.

I followed the two prisoners to a bathroom. It had a big cement tub surrounded by ten black rubber basins. The window that should have been covered with plastic was bare, so the room was the same temperature as the outside. The only things on the wall were two lines of nails for hanging clothes. The room also had forty rubber face bowls.

One prisoner handed me prison clothing. Although everything in my life had been upside down, I couldn't believe what I saw. I was so stunned, I didn't know what to do. I thought I was hallucinating. The clothes were like stiff leather from stains of sweat and dirt. I asked myself, *How could anyone put that on their body? These are not clothes.*

In panic, I dropped the clothes. Tears poured out of my eyes.

The prisoners urged me to put them on. They said that if I took a long time, the officer would get mad at them. Finally, I put them on. Although I came to the prison at the end of November, I was given only a quilted, cotton undershirt and pants to last all winter. The cotton in the shirt and pants was lumpy and old. The colors in the clothing were faded and the cloth was oily from being unwashed so long. At first, the stiff clothing irritated my skin. My toes stuck out of the old, worn-out cotton, Korean-style socks. Suddenly, I felt as if I had changed from a human into a wild animal.

I followed a prisoner into a hallway of dark cells. Each cell had one window and one door. The tops of the doors had tags with the factory's name and the cell number. In the middle of each door was a hole the size of a small rice bowl. The hole was used for communicating and for passing food and supplies such as toilet tissue or feminine products into the cell. In emergency situations, prisoners called to an official through the hole.

I stood before my cell. It was named "Newcomer's cell." It had a small window, a toilet, and a cabinet in the corner. When I entered the cell, I had to remove my shoes and put them on the cabinet. I saw a

A framed copy of the Prisoners' Commandments was hanging on the wall of the cell. Below that were hanging small packs of toothbrushes and toothpaste. The prisoners shared combs. Each cell also had a speaker to listen to radio programs.

framed copy of the Prisoners' Commandments hanging on the wall. Below that hung small packs of toiletries containing only a toothbrush and powdered toothpaste. The prisoners shared combs.

The Prisoners' Commandments

I found out that when prisoners first came to the prison, they stayed in the newcomers' cells for about two weeks. The cells were cold because winter air blew in from cracks in the wooden floor. It was almost as cold inside as it was outside. There was one heating system in the cell area, but the officers hardly ever turned it on because they wanted to save coal. The only time the heating system came on was for an hour around 1 a.m. after the prisoners returned from work. But the officers' work area had a good heating system in the floor. Prisoners came to stoke the fireplace every hour.

Each cell had a speaker with which prisoners listened to the Central Party's radio programs. The prisoners were required to attend a class where they reviewed monthly magazines published by the National Security Department. During the stay, the new prisoners had to memorize the Prisoners' Commandments and learn prison policy. The Commandments were divided into three parts:

1. Adore the authorities of Kim Il Sung and Kim Jong Il with all your heart. If you find any factor hurting their authority, you should fight it until death.

2. All prisoners will participate in the labor assembly line and complete their daily, monthly, and seasonal quota. While you are working, do not waste or destroy materials.

3. All prisoners should obey prison policy. Everyone should move as a group. No individual behavior is allowed. No one can leave during work hours. No talking, laughing, or singing is allowed. When an officer calls, the prisoners should come quickly before him and sit on their knees. Keep your conditions sanitary. Whoever breaks the policy will be severely punished.

After the new prisoners memorized the Prisoners' Commandments, they were given the task of keeping up the grounds.

One of the hardest rules for new prisoners to obey was not being able to relieve themselves. The prisoners got up at 5 a.m. and went to bed at 12:30 a.m. During work hours, they could go to the toilet only three times. There were no exceptions. Some of the new prisoners wet their pants.

Crimes of Ordinary People

There were about forty people in the newcomers' cells. About ten new prisoners arrived every day. If the cells became too crowded, prisoners were moved out before their time was up.

When I entered the prison at the end of the year, the prisoners were under heavy pressure to complete their annual factory production quota. The new prisoners were given a pile of military coats and ordered to put buttons on them. Under the dim light, the prisoners constantly pricked their fingers with the needles. The new prisoners had to finish their job and memorize the Prisoners' Commandments to pass the officer's inspection.

Before my arrest, I used to regard prisoners as human trash. But 80 percent of the women in this prison were housewives. Since the 1980s, when the North Korean economy began declining, crime has increased. These women had watched their children starve. When they tried to steal food, they were arrested. Too many of these women, who were supposedly loved by their husbands and children, became criminals because of society's illness.

One thirty-nine-year-old woman was named Young Hee Kim. While she worked as a sales clerk, she stole one kilogram of sugar and sold it. After an inspector discovered it, she was sentenced to three years in prison and her property was confiscated. She thought the trial was unfair, so she appealed to a higher court. But because her action angered the public prosecutor, he extended her sentence to twenty years.

Two ladies from Hwe-Ryung City in North Ham-Kyung Province were named Jung Ok Kim and Sung Il Kim. Their husbands were miners—one of the lowest paying jobs in North Korea—so their husbands could barely support their families. When these two women could no longer stand watching their children starve, they sneaked into a threshing factory to steal a pack of corn. Unfortunately, they were caught.

As Jung Ok Kim stood before the court, she complained, "Do you think I should have starved to death and not stolen anything? Don't you understand? I didn't want to steal. But I had to do it because the government didn't give me anything to eat and my children are starving to death. It's so hard to live in North Korea right now." Her complaint was considered as an insult to the government so she was sentenced to fifteen years of imprisonment.

I met a mother and daughter from Anju City in South Pyong-An Province who were also sentenced to fifteen years. The eighteen-year-old daughter, Young Hee Go, hacked to pieces the neck of her sleeping father because he ate too much.

Most of the prisoners had very grave faces because they worried about their families and their future. Because most of them had gone through the interrogation process, their bodies were very frail. Then they received too little food to sustain their weakened bodies. They were supposed to get 700 grams of food daily, of which about 60 percent was corn, 30 percent beans, and 10 percent rice. But the rice and beans were taken by the officers, so the prisoners had only corn and salty cabbage soup all year round. Consequently, prisoners received less than 300 grams of food per day—only 100 grams (3.5 ounces) of food per meal. On top of that, if a prisoner broke prison policy, the amount of their food was decreased.

The starvation and cold were the hardest things for new prisoners to endure. They initially received only 80 grams per meal, which is not even one mouthful. While I was in the newcomers' cell, I figured that the prisoners who were working in the factory were given a big meal—700 grams a day.

The new prisoners were not allowed to talk. They had to sit on their knees with heads bowed until an officer said, "Relax." From time to time, an officer would come into the cell block and yell, "Who did the talking? Do you all want to go to solitary confinement?"

A couple of days after each new prisoner arrived, she was interviewed by an officer. He questioned what the prisoner did before coming to prison. Then one by one, each prisoner was assigned to a factory according to her skills.

I was in the newcomers' cell for only ten days. This short time was my dark introduction to the inhuman world of the prison.

Chapter 7

ALTHOUGH THEY WORKED THEIR HARDEST...

KHECHEN PRISON CONSISTED OF ELEVEN departments, including a personal goods production factory, export department, shoe production factory, garment production, garment cutting factory, design (machinery preparation), facility services, and disciplinary department (a prisoner who broke policy was sent here for punishment). Each department had 250 to 300 prisoners.

By organizing prisoners into groups, a few officers were able to control many prisoners. Each department was divided into five units of fifty to sixty prisoners, with each unit divided into ten teams of five to seven prisoners. Each department had a supervisor, record keeper, and messenger. Each unit and team had a foreman. The supervisors were responsible for leading a group and keeping prisoners from breaking policy. The record keepers were responsible for tracking incoming and outgoing materials. The messengers distributed and collected daily quotas and controlled production. The unit foremen were in charge of managing production plans and quotas along with unit discipline. Team leaders controlled team member activity.

Prisoners had the hardest time adjusting to one rule in the Prisoners' Commandments: "Everyone moves as a group." Whenever a newcomer joined a team, everyone on the team suffered because if one prisoner broke policy, the whole team was punished. Therefore, team leaders were especially strict on newcomers. Everyone had to eat, sleep, work, or use the toilet at the same time. For example, until the team was called to use the toilet, team members could not relieve themselves. So new prisoners often wet their pants. Other team members understood what she was going through because the same thing happened to them.

About three hundred people shared one toilet at each factory, so three to four prisoners had to use the small toilet at one time. (The toilets used in North Korea are not same as in the United States. They have a much larger hole so that four can share.) Each toilet was guarded by prisoners who were assigned that task. The toilet attendants had to stay in the smelly room for seventeen to eighteen hours each day. They were usually handicapped or prisoners with long sentences. Because they breathed the terrible stench and suffered from the severe malnutrition of prison, their faces were swollen and turned bright yellow. It was awful to look at their faces. They usually did not live very long.

Most prisoners worked very hard to complete their work quota. If they didn't, they received a smaller food ration. Because prisoners were afraid of a reduction of even a small amount of rice, they risked their lives to meet their daily quota. However, the prisoners with toilet assignments had no quota to meet. They received the full amount of food with extra salted soup, unless they broke policy.

At 5:30 a.m. the messenger distributed quotas to each prisoner. At 11 p.m., the messenger gathered them back and examined each prisoner's activity to see if they met their quota. Prisoners who could not complete their job had their food reduced to 240 grams (8.4 ounces) for one day of incomplete work, and 210 grams (7.4 ounces) after four days of incomplete work. If a prisoner broke policy by laughing, singing, looking at her reflection in a glass, or breaking the machinery, she was sent to solitary confinement for seven to ten days. Prisoners in solitary confinement received only 90 grams (3.2 ounces) of food per day.

The fear of starvation made people persevere supernaturally. Prisoners considered it so important to finish their job and receive the full portion of food that nothing hindered them from trying. When one prisoner's finger was bleeding after being pierced by a sewing machine needle, she just put sewing machine oil on her finger and continued working. One person had a very high fever, but she did not stop working. The environment turned human beings into animals that fight for food until death. The prisoners' only hope was to survive until the last day of their sentence so they could return to their families. They knew that if they died in prison, their body would be thrown into the mountains and eaten by wild animals.

The prisoners truly cared for each other because they were all in the same boat. Most of them were innocent of their crimes, and they knew they could die at any time. They survived every minute with fear. After a day of heavy labor, they had only four hours of sleep from 1 to 5 a.m.; however, they could not relax even during these four hours. Every night, two prisoners were assigned to watch the others who slept. The next morning, the prisoners who stayed awake had to report what the other prisoners said in their sleep. Therefore, prisoners had to be alert even while they slept.

The cells in which eighty to ninety prisoners slept were very small— only 6 meters (19.7 feet) long by 5 meters (16.4 feet) wide. Each cell also had a toilet, so the actual sleeping area for all the prisoners was even less. It was torture to sleep with so many people in a small cell. Prisoners laid down and put their clothes under their heads. One would put her feet to the east and the next would put her feet toward the west, so that all the prisoners' faces were surrounded by the smelly feet of nearby prisoners.

It was especially terrible to sleep during the summertime with so many sweaty people laying so close together. The heat from their bodies made the cell hotter. Prisoners hated to come back to the cells. They would rather sleep in the factory for two hours than come back. However, in the winter it was nice to sleep with so many people since their bodies kept each other warm.

My First Day in the Factory

On December 1, 1987, I completed ten days of newcomer orientation and was dispatched to the personal goods production factory. At 8 a.m., I was led into a two-story factory along with twenty other newcomers. We arrived at a black iron gate.

At the cell guard's signal, the door-control prisoner opened the door. When we entered, another guard searched our bodies. All we had were two bowls and a pack for our toothbrush and toothpaste, so the search was done quickly. As I entered the factory, I saw about seventy to eighty electric sewing machines where prisoners were quilting military coats. Prisoners on one side were making cloth bags; those on the other side were making belts, gun covers, military dog's muzzles, shoe supports, and so on.

At the entrance to the factory was an office made of glass, with an inspection desk located about five meters away from the office.

I arrived at the factory near the end of the year, so everyone was busy trying to complete the annual quota—10,000 coats. There were four steps: quilting the coats, sewing on buttons, trimming the thread, and passing inspection. Then five completed coats were bound together to be shipped out. The prisoners were working night and day. For the past month, they had slept only two hours a night at their work spots.

Since the factory light was so dim, prisoners had to work by the tiny light bulb on their sewing machine. The prisoners worked so frantically that their eyebrows were covered with cotton dust. Often they could not see far because the cotton dust covered their eyes. Their clothing was stained with sweat and sewing machine oil. Their clothes were ripped, but they didn't have time to patch them. They worked without any feeling or expression on their faces, which were yellow from not enough sunshine. It was difficult to tell whether they were men or women or even human. They looked like a group of ghosts—creatures that exist only in horror stories.

I was assigned to sew twenty buttons on each coat. An officer told me that he was very lenient and would give me only seven hundred buttons to put on that day. However, it was hard to sew the buttons on the thick cotton coats. Although I tried my best, I could not complete the job. None of the other newcomers completed their jobs either.

The next morning, my supervisor reported my failure to complete my quota to the managing officer, and he got upset, ordering my food reduced for a day. My expectation of eating a decent meal in the prison disappeared, and the severe reality hit me. It was going to be dreadful to survive for thirteen years like this. Once again my body shook with anger toward the police chief who was responsible for my "crime" and imprisonment.

Factory Work and the Workers

The next morning at 4 a.m., the guards dispatched all newcomers to put cotton stuffing into the coats. Prisoners worked nineteen hours a day

The prisoners worked frantically and were covered with cotton dust.

without taking a single break. It was so dark that I could not even distinguish what was in front of me. My thin, stiff uniform could not protect me from the cold air in the factory.

Officers treated us like animals. They never explained to us what to do, but communicated with the prisoners by whipping, kicking, and cursing. While prisoners were being beaten, they couldn't stop working or look back at the officers. If a prisoner moaned or tried to avoid getting hit, she was put into solitary confinement, the worst punishment in prison. The solitary confinement cell was only high enough to allow a person to sit on the floor. Concrete thorns stuck out of the walls so the prisoner could not lean against them. The person could only sit and not move for many days. If prisoners were consigned to solitary confinement during the winter, their legs became paralyzed.

Instead of pure cotton, the factory used reconditioned cotton and scraps of fabric to stuff the coats. I thought, *Whoever wears these coats will be wearing dust on his body.* To get the cotton into the clothes, I pounded on the big ball of cotton with three long wooden sticks to flatten it.

My feet were cold while I was working, so I covered them with a piece of fabric and wrapped my waist with a cotton burlap bag. The working prisoners were covered with dust, and the burlap bags looked so grim. Seventeen hours of pounding on cotton caused me to breathe in a great amount of dust. After work, I felt very stuffy, and black cotton came out when I blew my nose.

It was common to find all kinds of things in the used stuffing, such as nails, pieces of iron, buttons, or needles. One night, an old lady named Chun Hwa Kim accidentally put a nail into a coat while she was stuffing it with cotton. When the next prisoner quilted the coat, her sewing machine needle broke when it hit the nail. Chun Hwa Kim was sent to solitary confinement for allowing the nail in the coat.

Chun Hwa Kim was from Gusung City. She had been unjustly arrested for operating a side business. This is why it all happened. In 1984, after Kim Il Sung returned from a trip to Europe, he permitted people to start small businesses with rice cakes, bean curds, and motels. Within three years, these businesses became the livelihood for many living in Gusung City. But Kim Jong Il, son of Kim Il Sung, thought that the business owners were adopting capitalism, so he strictly controlled any kind of business. Many housewives were arrested just for doing what Kim Il Sung allowed them to do. Chun Hwa Kim was one of them. She told me that she had a handicapped husband who was injured during the Korean conflict and two daughters at home. She worried about her daughters marrying because people often wanted nothing to do with the family of a criminal.

After a year in prison, her body was too weak to survive solitary confinement. When Chun Hwa Kim was released from solitary confinement, she could not use her calf muscles. She had to almost crawl on the ground when she went somewhere.

Her legs got worse and worse until finally they were completely paralyzed. Yet she worked on. But the officers, especially one twenty-four-year-old woman, did not stop beating her. Chun Hwa Kim was beaten and starved for a month. Finally, she died one night on the cold factory floor. Her team leader reported her death to an officer. She responded, "That's fine. She wasn't worth anything anyway. I guess we have to waste two blankets to wrap up her dead body."

I thought that the officer's voice sounded evil. The officer yelled at the prisoners not to look at the dead body because that might affect their productivity. A little later, two prisoners came with blankets and took the body out. That was the first time I witnessed a death in prison, but it was not the last one I had to watch. A lot of housewives died in the factory and were thrown out into the mountains.

The New Lunar Year; the New Horrors

As the lunar new year came, the coat production ended. Then both male and female prisoners were drafted to carry fertile soil down the mountains to a corn field. The mountain was 600 meters (1,970 feet) high, steep, and slippery. The mountain had two roads—one for male prisoners and the other for female prisoners, to separate them. After the prisoners climbed the mountain, they loaded soil into their carrier and came back down. They had to walk single file because the road was so narrow. Everyone had to carry 20 kilograms (44 pounds), and if a prisoner had less, the officer kicked him.

Prisoners climbed the mountain six times a day, three times in the morning and three times in the afternoon. The prisoners had to walk backwards as they came down, because if they walked forward with the heavy soil on their backs, the weight would cause them to roll over. The work was very hard. As we walked up the mountain, we became breathless and felt like our stomachs were being torn apart.

Almost all officers and guards were called for duty to prevent any escape. About 650 officers and soldiers lined the mountain road from the bottom to the top. They pointed their guns toward the prisoners, watching for anyone who would try to run away. If a guard suspected anyone was planning to escape, he would shoot instantly.

In the middle of January 1988, the prisoners were exhausted from climbing the mountain so many times. That afternoon, something tragic happened. While the prisoners were carrying soil down the mountain on their backs, one female prisoner slipped on the gravel and fell. Her carrier came off and hit two prisoners below her. All three of the women fell down a cliff. As soon as a guard found them, he shot them. It all happened so quickly that I was very shocked. The guard who shot the women arrogantly told the rest of us, "If you aren't careful, you'll end up like that."

That evening, the prisoners returned to the prison and the dead bodies were abandoned in the mountains. When morning came, I was afraid to go back to the mountain. While I was walking to the mountain, I doubted that I would ever get out of prison. When I passed the spot where the three prisoners had been killed, I saw only blood; their dead bodies were gone. I guessed that male prisoners had taken them away. No one ever mentioned the incident because it was so horrible.

The Hardest Jobs

I was sent back to work for about three months in the personal goods production factory. The officers changed my job every three to four days. Whenever I got used to doing a job, I had to learn another. If the officers had let me get used to the production, I would have learned the technique and exceeded the daily quota, but they never allowed me to stay long. I made a lot of things: bags, gun covers, and belts.

I was usually assigned the hardest jobs of all the newcomers. One time, I had to inspect 500 to 600 leather products such as belts and bags. After I inspected them, an officer looked at a few of the products to see how I did. If he did not find any flaws, he gave me a stamp to put on the products. If he found something wrong, he beat me. The inspector was about thirty years old, and at each inspection, he kicked me instead of telling me what to do. I decided he would get sick if he didn't kick someone. So I always had bruises all over my body.

One time he sarcastically said, "You are too smart to be here. What brought you here?" Then he kicked me for no reason. I could not stand the fact that someone younger than me, who should respect an older person and use honorary words, was abusing me. He was not showing me any respect as an elder. I will never forget how that younger man insulted and humiliated me like that.

The hardest job at the factory was making the belts. My job was punching holes and putting nails on 120 thick leather belts. Working with the heavy leather was very difficult. I became sweaty and my wrists and shoulders ached.

I took off my old worn-out shoes, since they came off all the time, and walked around in bare feet. The first few days, my feet bled and I had blisters all over. However, I got used to walking barefoot.

After living a couple of months in prison, I began to learn how to survive. That meant becoming more skillful than other prisoners. Whatever kind of job I was given, I did my best to complete it. When I was dyeing the clothes, for example, I had to be very alert. If I would put the clothes into the dye in the wrong order, the color would come out wrong and I would be put into solitary confinement. Sometimes I distributed material to tailors in the right order. That job was pretty confusing, but I did it without making a single mistake. An officer watching me asked, "Have you done this job before?"

"No," I answered.

He complemented me. "Wow! You are very good at that. I have never seen anyone do this better than you. I think the chief officers picked the right person."

At the time, I didn't understand his comment. I learned later that when the newcomers were interviewed by an officer, he tried to find out what they could do. I had had an interview with the chief officer who learned that I had once been an accountant. He wanted to know whether I could handle an accounting job in prison. For this reason, my previous experience would soon bring me to the export factory.

Chapter 8

Export Factories—The World's Worst Slavery

On March 10, 1988, four months after I arrived in prison, I still had not gotten used to the environment. A warden summoned me to her office. Although I had seen her from a distance, I had never been close to such a high officer, so I was very afraid to meet her. She looked about fifty years old. Like all other prisoners who come before officers or guards, I knelt down on the dirty floor with my head bowed to answer her questions.

She asked me about my experiences in society. She said, "We're going to open an export factory in a short time. I want you to be the record keeper for the factory. This means that we trust you, and you must do your best to give the greatest benefit to the government."

When I walked out of the office, a lady named Chang Yu Han came up to me. I ignored her because prisoners are not supposed to talk to each other. Chang Yu Han had a twenty-year sentence, and she had been in prison for ten years. During that time, she had gotten smaller in stature. She said her height used to be 158 centimeters (5.2 feet), but ten years later she was only 140 centimeters (4.6 feet). She had a lump on her shoulder so she always turned her head to one side. Whenever I looked at her silhouette at night, she looked like a monster. She said,

"You are really lucky to be picked by the officer. I bet you can get out of here alive."

Early the next morning before the prisoners left for the factory, an officer called out a list of prisoners' names. Prisoners who heard their names packed their things and walked out of their cells into the hallway. That morning, there were about three hundred prisoners sitting on their knees in the hallway. They had been called out to work in the export factory.

A high-ranking female officer was put in charge of the export factory. She was the oldest female officer. Since she would retire in a year, she was happy that she could show her loyalty to the Party by earning greater foreign currency before she retired. Thus, she placed harder production requirements on the prisoners.

Starting in May 1988, the export factory began producing women's brassieres to export to Russia. I heard that Russia paid two dollars per brassiere. The fabric and thread were very high quality. Officers told us that Russia had very strict inspections so the garments would give the best comfort to the women's breasts, therefore the prisoners had to work carefully on them. Over the next six months, the prisoners in the export factory produced 900,000 brassieres.

About that time, I began to get upset with the North Korean government. I thought, *Russia's government is making such soft, comfortable brassieres for women, but North Korea's government is arresting innocent housewives and treating them worse than animals.* This was about the time I began to wake up from my brainwashed Communist ideas.

The export factory also produced doilies to export to Poland. Prisoners stitched a ginseng pattern on the doilies. Officers urged prisoners to work faster to meet the shipping date. Since stitching was a new skill for most prisoners, a lot of inferior goods were produced. If a prisoner ruined a product, she was accused of wasting the government's money and she was given only 80 grams of corn to eat. An average of forty to fifty prisoners per day received reduced food rations.

In January 1990, a second export factory was opened. It received an order from Japan for hand-knit sweaters. As prisoners began to knit the sweaters, their unsanitary conditions became a problem. While they knitted, their dirty hands tainted the yarn. Officers brought soap and basins and ordered the prisoners to wash their hands. Prisoners also covered their legs with white fabric to protect the yarn from getting dirty. But Japan still complained about unclean sweaters. Consequently, the officers ordered the prisoners to wash their hands more often. But the prisoners were too busy to wash their hands many times a day because they had to complete a sweater every three days. Sometimes, to save time, the prisoners didn't go to the toilet. That year, tens of thousands of sweaters were shipped to Japan.

Conditions in the Export Factory

The prisoners in the export factory were treated even worse than those in the other factories. Our days were a series of unendurable labor. Getting kicked and slapped was common. The female prisoners got used to an officer's kick or a slap on the face. After a few years of little food, no sunshine, constant beatings, and demanding work, prisoners began to lose the strength in their backbones. As the spine weakened, ligaments started popping out at the back of their necks. The prisoners became ugly, like beasts. The export production was the fruit of unbelievable human abuse. Yet in the midst of abuse and cursing, millions of products were made, wrapped, and delivered to the Nampo Port to meet the deadlines.

At midnight, a bell rang to signal the end of the day. The fatigued prisoners just sat at their work stations because they were too weak to stand for even a minute.

When the prisoners sewed with white fabric, they had to be careful because the sewing machine oil would get it dirty. If someone made a small spot on a product, she was beaten until she lost consciousness. If prisoners continuously made mistakes sewing doilies, they were placed in solitary confinement.

When a prisoner broke the policies, she had to write a document that criticized herself before she was sent to solitary confinement. The solitary confinement room, nicknamed "the room to meet death," was located at the end of the first floor. It was very small—only .6 meters (2 feet) wide and 1.1 meters (3.6 feet) high. The prisoner had to crawl into the confinement cell and could not stand or lay down. She was sealed in with iron bars. Because prisoners could not move, often their legs would become paralyzed.

A hole in the floor was used as a toilet. In the winter, cold air from the toilet hole froze the prisoners and they came out with frost bite. In the summer, thousands of maggots crawled out of the hole, so the prisoner had to pick up the maggots and put them back into the hole.

Prisoners in solitary confinement were given only 30 grams (1 ounce) of corn and a cup of salt soup at each meal. Once in a while, a rat crawled out of the hole in the floor. A rat was a cherished treasure for confined prisoners who would catch the rat and devour the "tasty" living animal. In fact, rats were the only kind of protein prisoners ever got. But a prisoner had to eat the rat secretly because if an officer found out, the prisoner was punished.

One forty-year-old lady named Man Ok Song was put in solitary confinement for seven days because she stained some fabric. Another time, Soon-Young Um, Eun-Hee Pak, Hwa-Sook Lee, and seven others were placed in solitary confinement for seven days. When they came out, their legs look like octopus legs. None of the women could stand alone.

One illiterate lady named Young Sook Kim was assigned to the knitting factory. She had no elementary education, so reading a knitting pattern was almost impossible for her. She tried to figure it out, but she kept tangling the yarn and pulling out her stitches until the yarn was ruined. She was so frustrated that she muttered through tears, "Why was I born in a rural town where I had no opportunity to go to school?"

An officer heard her crying. He kicked her and said, "Do you think I believe that you do not know how to read? I know you are trying to make excuses not to work!"

She answered desperately, "I really don't know how to read or write."

He kicked her and beat her some more. "Our government eliminated all illiteracy a long time ago. And you are saying you are illiterate? I'll have to drag this liar to the interrogation office."

The next day she was dragged into the interrogation office, which was used for questioning and torturing prisoners. A month went by, but Young Sook Kim never returned from the interrogation office. A prisoner later told me that she had been beaten to death.

With a broken heart, I remembered my friend. She once told me that she came from a town in the mountains. It was called "the closest town to the sky." Young Sook Kim couldn't go to school because it was too far away from where she lived.

After Young Sook Kim died, her husband sent her a letter. He didn't know about his wife's death. His letter said that he offered wild ginseng to Kim Il Sung with a wish for his long life. Wild ginseng is a very precious tonic medicine that is extremely hard to find in the mountains. It is worth much more than cultivated ginseng.

An officer read the husband's letter to the prisoners. "While you are not appreciating the government and being lazy, your families are devoted to the government and Kim Il Sung."

I thought, *I wonder whether Young Sook Kim's husband will still be devoted to Kim Il Sung after he finds out how his wife died.*

"Earning in Hell"

In 1990, the export factory obtained more orders from other countries. The Khechen prison warden and the rehabilitation officer were overly eager to earn foreign currency. Every day the warden came to the export factory and constantly threatened the prisoners: "If you ruin a product, I will put you in solitary confinement."

One time France ordered paper roses. Prisoners rolled different colored papers to make golden, silver, and spotted roses, then tied them onto sticks. Each prisoner had a quota of 1,000 roses per day. After rolling that many roses, their fingertips were worn out and blood oozed from the skin. But once the quota is set, it must be fulfilled. That meant that each hour, 60 roses had to be made to keep up with the quota—one every minute. To save time, prisoners often hurried to the toilet and ate their balls of rice while they worked.

When the export factory first opened, the officers chose relatively young and healthy prisoners for the work. Two years later, many of these prisoners had become handicapped or had died from suffering under heavy labor, beatings, and all kinds of punishments. The central public security director urged the prisoners to make more and more goods. Consequently, the Khechen prison earned a great deal of foreign currency with the free labor, so the government promoted even more export production. With the money they earned, the officers imported television sets and refrigerators. These were given to each district security bureau officer and called "presents from Kim Il Sung."

I thought about the foreigners who would buy what the prisoners in North Korea had made. They would never know that the products they purchased were made in exchange for a prisoner's life. They wouldn't know that the products were made in a prison where all kinds of bacteria and viruses are rampant. And that among the prisoners, earning foreign currency was called "earning in hell."

My Long Days in Solitary Confinement

In November 1989, I was assigned to solitary confinement. At that time, prisoners were making costumes for the International Youth Festival held in Pyongyang. Right before the costumes had to be shipped out, I discovered that one costume was missing. I quickly made a replacement with leftover fabric and shipped it out. Later, an officer found the missing costume under the chair of one of the tailors. Her name was Young Sun Suh. She had accidentally ruined the costume, so she hid it to avoid punishment.

The foreman of her unit, Myung Hee Hwang, and I were considered responsible for her crime so we were sent to solitary confinement.

One officer said of Young Sun Suh, "Her behavior is contempt against the International Youth Festival and discredits Kim Il Sung's authority. This is an anti-Communist act." Young Sun Suh was sent to the interrogation office.

Before Young Sun Suh became a prisoner, she had worked as a cook for construction workers. She was so sweet and nice to everyone. The construction workers asked her for more rice, so she cooked more for them. At the end of the month, the supply of rice was considerably less, so she was accused of stealing.

In the interrogation office, Young Sun Suh was so afraid of being tortured that she agreed to whatever the officer said. She was executed before everyone's eyes in May 1990. It was not easy to forget her even after her death.

Before Myung Hee Hwang and I were put into solitary confinement, we had to write a self-criticizing document. I wrote as one officer dictated, "With the care of Kim Il Sung, I had a life without any worry. Instead of giving my utmost loyalty to his care, I ungratefully betrayed him by breaking prison policy."

It made me very upset to write such nonsense as "with the care of Kim Il Sung, I had a life without worry," but I had to be silent and patient. As I stood there with a blank look, the rehabilitation section chief said, "Why are you standing there like that? You should be thankful that we let you live rather than kill you for your crime." After I finished writing, we came out of the office.

That night after a hard day of work, I was entering my cell when I heard my name being called for solitary confinement.

As I went, a cell control security officer, a short, stocky woman, said in a thick Northern accent, "Soon Ok! What's the matter? We especially trusted you and put you in a record keeping position. You were not supposed to break our trust like this. Now you're heading for solitary confinement." In reality, no matter how well the prisoners behaved, almost everyone in prison was sent to solitary confinement.

I entered the cold, dark confinement cell. Since the confinement cell is always dark, I had no idea how many days passed. The only way I could tell was by counting the number of meals I received. When my rice was brought in, I received only 30 grams, which amounted to only a spoonful. After one swallow, the rice was gone and I didn't feel as if any rice ever reached my stomach. After sitting in one position for so long, my hips and waist began to hurt, but I couldn't lean against the thorny wall.

One night, I saw something moving in the dim light. When I got closer, I found a mother rat with a baby in its mouth climbing the wall toward the ceiling. For a minute, I was totally absorbed by every movement of the rat. In my thrill to see the instincts of motherhood in the small animal, I forgot how hungry and cold I was. I thought, *Even these small animals take care of their babies, but we humans in this republic aren't allowed to take care of our own children.* I felt so miserable about living in a worse environment than the rat lived. I couldn't comprehend why any woman, especially a mother raising children, is brought to this terrible place to secretly cry when thinking of her own children. It was hard to accept this harsh reality.

I remembered the words to a North Korean song, "A woman is a flower of happiness. A woman is a flower of love in a family." But the women in Khechen prison were flowers of sadness who

The rat was carrying a baby in her mouth. For a minute, I was totally absorbed by her every movement.

cried for their children. They were withered and trampled flowers.

Finally, I was released from solitary confinement. The first few days, whenever I was required to walk, my legs gave way under me. Fortunately, I had a job in which I could walk around a lot so my legs gained strength. But many women who came out of solitary confinement and worked in the same spot all day never walked again.

The Bald Female Prisoners

When Myung Hee Hwang was released from solitary confinement, she was moved to the PoHwa factory, which was a shoe factory. It is also one of the hardest places in prison. If prisoners broke prison policy or did not meet the daily quota, they were sent to the shoe factory.

The shoe factory squeezed out the last drop of the prisoners' blood and sweat. Workers were required to produce 3,000 pairs of shoes every day, and each pair went through 58 steps—all done by hand. Pouring hot rubber into the mold and taking the dried rubber out of the mold were especially hard. Many shoes were hung over a big pot of boiling water.

The factory's doors and windows were tightly closed even on hot summer days because the officers said that the outside air caused bubbles to form in the shoe glue. The atmosphere felt like a sauna, and the air easily suffocated first-timers. The temperature must have been above 100 degrees. The sweaty prisoners always looked as if they had just stepped out of the shower. Because they lost a lot of water through sweating, the prisoners suffered from more severe malnutrition and they fainted easily. They were supposed to receive a bigger ration of salty soup, but they did not get the right amount. Many prisoners lost their hair because of inadequate diet. The shoe factory had more people die of malnutrition than any other factory in the prison.

The shoe factory prisoners were almost naked to endure the heat. Most of the women didn't wear shirts, and they did not even cover their breasts. Their naked bodies were discolored from terrible burns.

The heat and malnutrition caused many prisoners to have hernias, which caused a lot of bleeding. The prison recycled fabric female hygienic napkins and supplied them to shoe factory prisoners since they had the most hernias. Some prisoners died from severe blood loss. In fact, I knew about ten prisoners who bled to death.

The officer of the factory was a man about fifty-five years old. He loved to harass the prisoners. He carried a long, wooden stick, and he jabbed prisoners with it to see them react. He laughed while he watched the pain on their faces.

Suffering for No Reason

Myung Hee Hwang did not deserve to be in any prison—and certainly not the shoe factory. She had received special training in the army and had become a platoon lieutenant. After she was discharged from the army, she got a job in the international department of the Central Bank.

One day her boss, the Secretary of the Communist Party in that city who was responsible for the Central Bank, asked her to exchange North Korean currency for foreign currency. She did as her boss told her to do. In North Korea, many Central Party committee members took foreign currency out of the bank for exchange and pocketed the gain for their own use. As this practice became more prevalent, the government began to inspect the central committee members. Many were arrested. During a government inspection, it was discovered that foreign currency had been exchanged without the government's approval. Bank workers like Myung Hee Hwang, who only did the errands requested by the Secretary, were punished for collaborating with their bosses. The powerless workers became victims under the shadow of greedy, powerful superiors. These workers suffered, were tortured, and died for no reason.

Myung Hee Hwang suffered from the hard labor in the shoe factory. Whenever I saw her, she was being cursed by the officers. Her job was gluing rubber on the shoes, but she was not good at it. Eventually, she was sent into solitary confinement again, and this time her legs became crooked.

Food Poisoning

The kitchen has as many sanitary problems as the laundry room. In May 1988, the prison kitchen didn't have enough water to rinse the cabbage, which was covered with an agricultural chemical. The cooks made the soup without washing the cabbage. Consequently, hundreds of prisoners got food poisoning. They began to vomit and have diarrhea, which were deadly to the prisoners because they were already malnourished.

About 150 prisoners died from the food poisoning. That May was very hot, so the dead bodies quickly began to rot and stink. Some prisoners who passed out were carried out with the dead to an ever-growing

They were all buried under the fruit tree.

pile of bodies. Those prisoners died without any medical treatment.

I was one of the prisoners who got food poisoning. I was put into a room with other poisoned prisoners where I vomited and suffered from diarrhea like the rest. Finally, I lost consciousness. Then I heard a voice, "Heaven will protect you... You will be saved."

When I came to a few days later and opened my eyes, I saw dead people laying all around me. I crawled out screaming, "Get me out of here!"

The prisoners who worked in the medical department pulled me out. My survival was a miracle. I did not understand how I lived among so many dying people, but today I know that it was a miracle of God. God must have answered my mother's and grandmother's prayers.

The Fruit Tree

The officers kept the food poisoning incident secret and didn't allow anyone to talk about it. All the dead were buried together under a fruit tree. Some of the dead bodies were not even covered with a blanket when they were buried. The prisoners' families didn't know about their deaths, and no one kept track of where the bodies were buried. They disappeared as if they did not leave a trace of their lives.

I will always remember my friends who died during that terrible time. One was from Sinuju City in North Pyong-An Province. Kwang Ok Choi, sixty-two years old, was arrested a few days before her youngest daughter's wedding. When she went out to barter her fish for a blanket for her daughter, she was caught by a policeman. Because of her arrest, her daughter postponed the wedding. Kwang Ok Choi always told me that if she got out of prison, she would prepare a nice wedding for her daughter. Now she would never be able to do that.

Another friend, In Sook Kim from Jae-Ryung City in North Hwanghe Province, said that she had lived with her three young children after her husband stepped on a land mine and was killed in the explosion. Every night in her prison cell, she called her children's names in her sleep.

I also remember another woman who always worried about her elderly mother. And there was an eighteen-year-old woman whose life was ready to bloom. They were all buried under the fruit tree.

After North Korea is united with South Korea, I will insist on going to that spot and digging under that fruit tree. People will see so many bones belonging to prisoners who had the most sorrowful life in the world. The barbarous crimes of the North Korean government will never escape the severest judgment of God and history.

Chapter 9

Dying Was Easier Than Living

LIVING WAS ALMOST LIKE TORTURE IN the prison. When I worked at the general staff office, all the high officers would stop by. There I heard all kinds of accounts of executions, punishments, and accidents. The officers regarded the lives of prisoners to be of less value than that of flies.

Prisoners were manipulated by officers who barked orders at us. It was much easier for the female prisoners to tolerate the abuse than the male prisoners, who had a hard time bearing up under the inhumane treatment. In the prison, there is never a trial for public execution or for an extension of sentences. Usually, the warden made the decisions. When male prisoners were beaten, some of them screamed and defiantly asked the officers to just kill them. These prisoners were treated as if they were anti-Communists who were dissatisfied with the Party. The officers publicly executed these prisoners.

In September 1990, when a group of prisoners harvested corn, five hungry male prisoners devoured some of the corn. As soon as an officer discovered them eating, he shot them.

Sometimes officers would watch a prisoner's death as if they were watching a funny show. Once, the officers gathered all the male prisoners in the yard and announced, "Whoever goes over the fence is free."

Many prisoners ran for freedom only to have their bodies scorched when they touched the high-voltage wire on the fence. The officers laughed at the dead prisoners. I thought, *Those officers are human out-*

side, but only evil inside.

In 1988, seven male prisoners and one female prisoner were executed without a trial. All six thousand male and female prisoners were required to watch. Each prisoner was tied to a post and his mouth covered with a mask. His eyes were wide open. Then six soldiers shot eighteen bullets into the upper part of the prisoner's body. Blood spurted out all over. One of the bodies was cut into two pieces by the bullets. Then an officer ordered all six thousand prisoners to walk around the body within three feet and look straight at it.

The officer said, "Look at him and feel hatred for him. Swear to yourself that you won't follow his example."

After each prisoner was shot, the officer who was second in command stood up and explained why the prisoner was executed. For one of the prisoners, the officer said, "He was against the government and dissatisfied with the Party policy, so he sneaked into the kitchen and stole balls of rice. While he was being punished for his crime of stealing, he said, 'I'd rather die than live in this pain.' His remark showed that he betrayed the great care of Kim Il Sung."

In prison, there was an intelligent man who invented a lot of things. His inventions helped the prison factory save money. Before he was sent to prison, he had graduated from an industrial college and used to work for the government.

One day he was walking by a department store when he heard someone yelling, "Stop! Thief!" Instantly he ran after the thief and pushed him. The thief fell down and hit his head and died on the spot. For this, the inventor was convicted of murder and sent to prison.

While in prison, he was always under heavy pressure to invent things for the prison officers. Unfortunately, one time his experiment failed. The officers defined his failure as an intentional waste of government money, so they dragged him to the interrogation office.

As he was being tortured, he cried, "I'd rather die than live like this. Just kill me!" The officers complied and executed him.

After Working So Hard

Women also died by execution. One female prisoner, Wul Rung Choi, came from Sunchen City. She lived in China until the 1960s when China went through the Cultural Revolution, then moved to North Korea. Her husband had died when the mine in which he was working collapsed. Many of the mine workers were Christians. If a mother went to prison, her entire family was destroyed. The children usually wandered in the streets until they were sent to a concentration camp. In prison, Wul Rung Choi worried about her two young children at home.

One time while in prison, she mentioned that she regretted leaving China and an officer overheard her. A decision was made to execute her because her one regretful remark was considered betrayal of the Communist Party.

Wul Rung Choi did not know about her execution until the last minute. I learned about it when one officer told me to bring four of the masks that were used for executions. I became nervous because I knew someone would be shot that day.

When I passed by several officers, I heard them talking about Wul Rung Choi's execution. I couldn't believe my ears. My legs were shaky and I got goose bumps all over my body. Wul Rung Choi was my friend, and I was with her many times when she cried for her children. I was extremely distressed. I thought, *Her babies will always wait in vain for their mother to return.* Although I had been in the prison for nine months, this was the first female execution I had seen.

I went to her work place and hid myself. I saw her working busily to complete her quota without knowing that in moments she would be killed.

Soon after I brought the four masks to the officer, the emergency bell rang. Whenever the bell rang, every prisoner had to be outside in the prison yard within twenty minutes. When we had gathered, the officer who was second in command announced, "At this time we will execute Wul Rung Choi."

As soon as he finished his announcement, four soldiers dragged out Wul Rung Choi. They tied her body onto the post and covered her mouth with the mask. She struggled against the soldiers, but her body was helplessly bound.

"Boom, boom, boom." The sound of the guns broke everyone's hearts. I could not believe that she was executed simply because she worried about her children and regretted moving to North Korea instead of completely trusting and loving the government.

After her execution, the prisoners were forced to walk around her dead body. I saw that the bullets had gone through her chest to her back. Her flesh was all bloody and mangled. I remembered how she had

They tied her body to the post and covered her mouth with a mask.

worked so hard until just a few minutes ago. She believed the officers when they said, "If you work hard and do not get into trouble, we will set you free." She worked so hard to follow their words so that she could go back to her little babies. I just did not know how to accept the terrible world in which I lived.

The Interrogation Office and the Mental Hospital

One lady who came from Hamhung City did not have contact with her family after she came to prison. Her son was later placed in the same prison, but she didn't know it. The first time she saw him was in August 1988 when the emergency bell rang to summon all the prisoners. When she went into the prison yard, she saw her son tied to an execution post. He also was falsely accused and placed in prison. The only crime he committed was to go around the country to try to find out where his mother was. He did not have a permit to leave his town.

She did not want to witness her son's execution so she screamed and ripped her eyeballs out. Everything happened so quickly. Her eyeballs were hanging by tendons and they were swinging. It was sickening and tragic to watch.

She yelled, "It's my fault for bringing you into the world!"

A soldier dragged her into the interrogation office where she was secretly executed.

When the soldiers shot prisoners during public executions, blood spurted on the people in the front row. Some of the female prisoners lost their minds and became psychotic. They cried, laughed, sang, or fainted. Their reaction was considered as disagreement with the Party or a lack of a firm belief in communism.

Once, two ladies sang loudly after watching an execution. They were sent to the "mental hospital." The mental hospital had "electrical treatment," which was really electric torture. After public executions, all twenty solitary confinement cells were full of prisoners who reacted to the horror.

Some prisoners were sent to the interrogation office and tortured. After being severely beaten, the prisoners agreed to whatever the officers said. Once they agreed with the officers, they were either executed or given longer sentences.

Mung Ae Kim, who was just thirty-five, was a sewing machine repair woman. Once, she broke a sewing machine while she was repairing it.

For that, she was confined in the interrogation office for three months.

After she was released, I saw that her body had frostbite all over it. She could not walk anymore.

Another female prisoner, assigned to do field work, sneaked into a field and pulled out one radish. She got caught. As a result, her sentence was extended five more years.

The Tragic Accidents

Accidents also took many lives. One summer day in 1990, the concrete ceiling of the sweater export factory collapsed. The accident happened because the old factory roof had cracks all over it. The officers didn't care about the safety of the prisoners so they didn't mend the roof. When it rained, water seeped into the cracks in the ceiling. Finally, the ceiling fell, killing or severely injuring about twenty female prisoners who were working under it.

As the prisoners under the concrete screamed, the warden yelled at them, "Shut up! If you make any more noise, I will squash your bodies!"

More officers came and kicked the injured prisoners to make them get back to work. Except for four prisoners whose brains were damaged or who had lost consciousness, all the injured prisoners were forced to return to work. The officers' only concern was that the accident might affect the shipping deadline.

As the warden left the scene, he said, "Don't sympathize with them." A few days later, one medical prisoner reported that the four brain-damaged prisoners were dead.

Another tragic accident also showed the little regard the prison officials had for the prisoners' welfare. The prison was divided by a 9-meter (30-foot) high fence. On one side were the male prisoners and on the other side were the females.

The ground around the fence had been dug out when the export factory was built close to the fence. The hole under the fence was never filled up again.

One spring day in 1990 at 11:30 a.m., half the fence fell down with a thunder-like sound. The falling fence knocked over a big pot of boiling glue in the shoe factory. About seven people were struck by the fence. The officers ordered the removal of the seven prisoners after the fence was quickly reconstructed. The dead bodies were as flat as jerky.

The bodies were buried under a tree as usual. The chestnuts on the trees were famous for their big size and good taste. There were also apple, pear, peach, and plum trees all over the mountains. The sweet fruits were good enough to be sent to the highest governors' houses. Until then, I did not know that burying dead bodies under trees produced good fruit.

One time I heard of a female prisoner who was involved in a horrible accident. When she pushed a cart into a big furnace, she tripped. Her left hand was completely cut off by the large cart. Although she didn't get any medical treatment, she survived.

Fleas feasted on the dirty, sweaty prisoners and sucked their blood until their skin had dark red bruises. It amazed me how many injured people remained alive under such unsanitary and harsh conditions.

I thought about humans. Sometimes they were extinguished so easily; sometimes they survived so incredibly. Based on man's miraculous survival, I could not deny the existence of God.

Chapter 10

TWISTING THE NECKS OF BABIES

IN 1989 AND 1992, THE PRISON WAS inundated by an epidemic called paratyphus from which I too suffered. This disease is related to colon bacillus, so drinking water or eating food makes the illness worse. The symptoms make people feel like the bottom of their stomach is twisted, and they have severe aches and a high fever twice a day. The body temperature usually reaches 102 to 105 degrees for two hours at a time. After their temperature goes down, people perspire and feel exhausted.

There was a medicine that could cure the illness, but the prison did not supply it Instead, the medical prisoners made a medicine with herbs, but it did not work.

In May 1989, paratyphus plagued a great number of prisoners. The sick could not continue working. A medical officer gave an order to put the sick prisoners in separate cells away from the well prisoners. About fifty were put into one cell. Some of them gained consciousness and were too sick and weary to call for help. They were too weak to pull themselves out of the pile of people. Even many of those who survived the disease died soon after their long, feeble struggle.

The officers refused to come close to the cell door because they were afraid of being infected by the prisoners. Therefore, the medical prisoners had to get rid of all the sick prisoners.

One seventeen-year-old girl had come to prison with her mother. She was infected with paratyphus and confined in the cell with me. As she lay next to me, her frail voice called out to her mother. "Mom! Apple...Mom! Water..." After longing for her mother and food, she finally stopped breathing. Since her mother worked in a different factory, she didn't know about her daughter's death.

The epidemic didn't abate until August. People were dying every minute. The three medical prisoners tried to separate the living from the dead, but three people could not handle many sick people. In addition, the smell of the dead bodies was terrible in the summer heat.

In spite of the bad circumstances, I survived the deadly illness. I was moved away from the dead bodies and confined with two other female prisoners. I was unconscious for many days. When I awoke, I was desperately thirsty because I didn't receive any water and I still had a high fever.

One of the two prisoners who lay beside me kept calling a man's name. A few days later, she stopped calling his name. I thought she was getting better, but that night I heard only the second prisoner's rough breathing. The second one swung her arms in the air and begged for food. None of the officers would approach the cell, so the medical prisoners sent in some corn to eat.

After many days had lapsed, I heard someone opening the cell door. It was a medical prisoner. She shook my body and said, "Wake up! The two others who are laying beside you are dead. I am amazed that you are still alive." Her voice echoed in my ears as if she were talking a mile away.

Miraculously, my fever went down and I began to recover. But the symptoms came back every May after that. As soon as I recovered enough to sit up, the officers gave me a lot of the work I couldn't do while I was sick for a month and a half. I looked at the mountain of work. The monthly closing report, cost accounting of material produced, production report, planning and variance report, and many others. I got mad at their selfishness.

In the Recovery Cell

A few days later, I was moved to a recovery cell. Six pregnant women were lying on the cold cement floor, which was not even covered with a mat. I thought, *Even animals receive better treatment outside this prison.*

The women were giving birth to their babies. The babies were supposed to be stillborn. Because Kim Il Sung had ordered that all anti-

Communists be eliminated within three generations, prison policy said that prisoners, who were considered anti-Communists, could not have babies in prison. When pregnant women came to prison, they were forced to abort their babies. Poison was injected into the babies cuddled in their mothers' wombs. After the injection, the pregnant woman suffered tremendous pain until the babies were stillborn about twenty-four hours later. Medical officers walked around the pregnant women and kicked their swollen bellies if they screamed or moaned.

Miraculously, some of the babies were born alive. They cried like normal babies do. When a live baby was born, a medical officer said to the medical prisoners, "Kill it! These criminals don't have any right to have babies. What are you doing? Kill it right now!"

The mothers of these newborn babies just laid on the floor and sobbed so helplessly while a medical prisoner's shaking hands twisted the baby's neck. Some of the women screamed and were beaten. The babies struggled for a short second, but they died so easily. Male prisoners wrapped the babies in rags and dumped them into a basket.

I was shocked. This was the most cruel human behavior I had ever seen in my life. Even today, I dream about the women who had just given birth to their babies. In my dream, they chase their babies. Often, the nightmare wakes me up.

I had a few friends who were medical prisoners. One time two of them came to see me. Their voices trembled, "It is the most evil thing. We just found out that the dead babies are used to make medicine."

Before they could say anything else, I covered their mouths with my hands. I said in a low voice, "I didn't hear what you said. Okay! I didn't hear you!"

I almost ran away from them. I was scared of being involved in gossip because the officers would kill me if they found out. At the same time, I was so bitter about living in such a hypocritical nation. I once believed Kim Il Sung and his doctrines. I was taught that people are the most important ingredient of our country and that our children are the future of the nation. But now I knew the real truth. Everything I learned was a lie to deceive the people. I began to hate the country I once loved.

The Tragedy of Hun Sik Kim

In June 1992, I got sick again. I ran a high fever and had chest pains. Suddenly, I couldn't walk or breathe. I was taken to a medical officer who diagnosed my condition as pleurisy. He said my chest cavity was filled with liquid. I figured that my disease was a result of the water torture in the interrogation center when my lungs were highly pressurized with water. After the torture, I remembered having the same type of pain, but it had healed itself. The pleurisy reoccurred because my body was getting so weak from malnutrition and heavy labor.

The officer didn't care how sick I was. He was just upset because I had to take time off of work.

It was August 1992, the hottest time of the year. I was put into a medical cell that I shared with Hun Sik Kim, who was once the principal of a high school. While she was a principal, she thought that the government required too much manual labor of her students and that the work was hindering their education. She sent a petition to the authorities expressing her opinion.

The government decided that she was rebelling against government policy. She was convicted of abusing her position by giving her students the impression that manual labor was worth less than studying.

In prison, Hun Sik Kim worked as a designer. As Kim Il Sung's birthday drew near, she was given a big project. Each year, all the government workers received a present from Kim Il Sung. That year's gift was a jacket made of imported nylon.

Hun Sik Kim designed the jacket. While she was working on it, she made a little mistake, but she found her mistake before the fabric was cut. She hadn't wasted any material.

But the officers accused her of intentionally delaying production. Right after the jacket project was completed, they sent her to solitary confinement for ten days. After she got out, she couldn't use her legs. Someone had to walk on either side of her to help her walk.

The officers thought she was faking her illness so they kicked her and cursed her. After a long time of physical abuse, her body got worse. Finally, she was carried to the medical cell and laid next to me. Still, the officers made her work.

A medical officer also doubted whether Hun Sik Kim was telling the truth about her illness. He decided to test her to see if her legs really were paralyzed. He brought two red-hot stones from the fire and put them on her hips. He said, "If you're faking, you will feel the heat and you will scream."

Hun Sik Kim heard and smelled her flesh burning, but her face didn't change. I was so furious that the medical officer would resort to such a barbarous testing method. My disgust and the smell of burning flesh made me dizzy.

I remembered my first day in this prison. Someone had told me that I was not human anymore and that I had to give up being human to survive. Now I completely understood what she had meant. I looked at Hun Sik Kim again. I still could not see any pain in her face while her flesh was burning.

After her hips were seared, Hun Sik Kim could no longer feel when she had to go to the bathroom. The hot summer sun deepened her sores. Soon pus and blood flowed from her hips.

Although I was suffering from a high fever, I couldn't just ignore her. I crawled to her and wiped her pus and covered her sores with a piece of fabric. As I did, she murmured, "I want to see the blue sky. My children are waiting for me." Tears flowed down her face. Since that day, I have never been able to erase the memory of her tears from my mind.

I grew sicker so I could not take care of her for many days. She moaned for several days. When I regained consciousness, I tore the fabric from her hips to see why she was moaning. As soon as I lifted the fabric, I screamed sharply. Hundreds of maggots were crawling on her hips, eating her flesh.

Hun Sik Kim continued to moan. The maggots began to crawl all over the cell. That night, Hun Sik Kim stopped breathing. I called for an officer through the hole on the door, "Sir, Hun Sik Kim is dead."

An officer yelled back at me, "Shut up! You filthy women! Why do you make noise at night? Her death is none of my business."

That night I shared the cell with her dead body. At daybreak, the dim sunshine exposed thousands of maggots in my cell. An officer saw the maggots through the hole in the door and said, "The maggots must have eaten up Hun Sik Kim!"

A medical prisoner brought me a bag to clean up the maggots. I swept them with my hands and put them into the bag. I was not afraid of the dead body, but I was afraid of my future becoming like hers. I swore to myself, "I cannot die like her. I must survive and tell the truth to the world!"

Back to the Recovery Cell

Perhaps because of my will power to live or because of God's protection,

I survived once again. And again I was sent to the recovery cell. That meant that I had to witness more pregnant women give birth to dead babies.

One medical prisoner told me that it is much harder to bear a dead baby than a living one. Since the pregnant women had just come from hard work at the factories, they didn't have enough strength to deliver babies. They were all so pale and drenched with sweat. They were not allowed to scream or make noise. If a woman moaned, a medical officer kicked her belly mercilessly. Some of them died as they delivered their dead babies.

I decided to stay outside in the hallway because I couldn't watch the cruelty. While I was in the hallway, a woman's cry drew my attention back to the cell. The woman was Bung Ok Kim. I knew her. She had married a man who was the only son in his family. His family had only had sons for five generations. Because Koreans still favor sons, having a son was a very crucial event in her family. Since the place where her husband worked didn't supply food, her family was starving. Finally, her mother-in-law had given her some aluminum pots to barter for food. Bung Ok Kim had left home without travel approval from the government.

While she was selling the pots, she was caught by a policeman. She received a three-year prison sentence and didn't even have a chance to go home and tell her family. Four months after she came to prison, she was forced to give premature birth to her baby. At that moment, she had just given birth to a live baby boy.

Bung Ok Kim begged a medical officer, "Sir! Please do not kill him! My mother-in-law is looking forward to seeing him. Please! Please! Don't kill him!"

Her eyes were burning with fire and she was extremely emotional. She cried because having a son meant prosperity, but having no son meant the extinction of the family line. This son meant so much to her. No one had protested like her before.

The medical officer panicked for a second, then quickly resumed his evil nature. He yelled, "Shut up! If you say one more word or open your mouth, I'll make you quiet forever!" He pitilessly kicked her stomach over and over. Then he called to a medical prisoner. "Hey! Come and twist the baby's neck!"

The baby died so easily and was thrown into a basket.

A chief medical officer came in and asked why it was so noisy. After the officer explained, the warden went to Bung Ok Kim and kicked her severely. Then he commanded that she be placed into solitary confinement.

I watched all this with shock and grief.

Five days after her baby's death, she died. Her cold body was abandoned in the solitary confinement cell. Because I worked in the general staff office, I had access to the prisoners' addresses. The next morning, I looked up her house address and memorized it. Before I left North Korea, I sent a letter to her family telling her story.

The Medicine of Death

One day, my medical prisoner friend Shin Ok Kim visited me. She and I were such good friends that we could discuss what was on our hearts. Whenever she wanted to talk to me, she volunteered to bring up the paper that I gave to the medical department every day. When she came, sometimes she cried and other times she sighed.

One day she said, "I know you will walk out of here, but I know I will never get out of here because I have killed too many people here in prison." Her voice quivered. "I thought that studying medicine would allow me to help save people's lives. I believed that I would be so happy to save them. But look at me! I'm using my knowledge to hurt people. I know I will never be forgiven." Her last words were, "Doctors are called only to save people, not to kill."

Not long before I was released from prison, she came to me with panic all over her face. She said that her medical prisoner friend, Myung Sook, had been dragged into the interrogation office because she had told people about using dead babies as medicine. Shin Ok Kim was shaking with fear for her friend.

I advised her, "Why did Myung Sook tell people? Didn't she know that we are not allowed to cry, laugh, or talk? She almost drove herself into this pit. And you listen to me. You have to be careful, too. Promise me that I will be the only person you talk to about this."

After Shin Ok Kim told me about her friend, I waited for Myung Sook to come back. But she never did; she was nowhere. Later a kitchen worker told me that she was no longer on the prisoners' list to cook for.

Chapter 11

Clay Was Tastier Than Rice

THE PRISON VALLEY HAD MANY PINE trees and the prison complex was surrounded by high and low mountains. After 1982 when more people were sent to the prison, the prisoners cultivated a corn field by cutting down pine and other trees on the hill. Because the hill was steep, it would not hold enough moisture in the ground and therefore did not produce adequately.

Prison officials decided to improve the soil on the hill. At the beginning of each year, they sent prisoners to carry soil from a river bank to the corn field. The young prisoners who had been in the prison for a short time and had not been as affected by malnutrition were sent to work outside the prison, as well as those who had all their body parts intact. Although the mountains protected the prison from civilian sight, the officers were still careful about exposing the deformed prisoners to outsiders. Less than twenty percent of the prisoners were considered "normal" enough to work outside the prison.

About four to five hundred female prisoners helped carry the soil. Whenever prisoners worked outside, all the officers and guards were armed with guns to watch for prisoners who might try to run away. Some of the guards looked out for outsiders who might trespass on the prison compound.

All the female prisoners wore white scarves, so they looked like a group of ducks. The officers called them "the duck heads." When they threatened the prisoners, they shouted, "Hey, duck heads! Don't even think about running away if you don't want bullets flying into your body."

The prisoners were instructed to follow a certain road. The female prisoners used the south road and the male prisoners used the north road. The south road was made of red clay and the north road of sand. A prisoner who stepped one foot off the road was immediately shot.

All for a Bag of Clay

One Sunday in late February 1990, the prisoners were called out to carry soil. That day, we had been given only a child's-fist-size ball of rice to eat. With all the hard work, we were exhausted and hungry. Carrying soil up the steep mountainside made us very thirsty, but the frozen mountain didn't offer us anything to eat or drink.

I usually worked with clothing factory prisoners when I was assigned outside work. While we dug the soil, we set aside the clay. I was too tired to pay attention to what was put aside.

Later when I returned to the river for more soil, one of the prisoners quickly handed me something. "Accounting prisoner," she said. "Do you want some too? Here! It is good. Taste it."

I looked at her, wondering where she got food.

She repeated, "It's pretty good. It tastes like rice cakes."

When I opened my hand, I discovered a ball of brown clay. Suddenly, I got upset because I thought she was joking. She saw my face getting red, so she and some other women encouraged me to eat the clay. "Put some in your mouth," they said. "It's delicious."

"How can people eat clay?" I asked.

"We already had quite a bit. It really fills you up."

Their arguments sounded good so I put a little bit of clay in my mouth. As they said, the clay did melt in my mouth so deliciously. That day, I ate about half a handful of clay. The clay filled my stomach, and I felt like it gave me energy. I melted the clay slowly in my mouth so I would not get caught by the officers.

That afternoon, the female prisoners were moved to the other side of the river. While they moved, they carried clay in a sack. When they arrived at the next spot, the male prisoners worked on the other side of the river. The men noticed the women eating clay. The men, who looked like living skeletons, kept signaling to send over some clay. But the

The clay did melt in my mouth so deliciously.

female prisoners ignored the signals because the guards were watching.

Suddenly, three male prisoners bolted to the other side of the river and snatched the clay sack. At that moment, a guard shot the three men. "Boom, boom, boom," the gun shots echoed in everyone's ear. We all turned to look at the three bleeding prisoners.

One of them was wounded in the abdomen. All his stomach organs came out. It was a hideous sight. He was still alive and he strained to say, "Help!"

I looked closer and saw that his intestines were caught by a corn stump. An officer came close to him and shot him three more times and said, "Go to hell."

Another guard yelled, "Hey! These two others are still alive."

The other two male prisoners were wounded in the leg. Red blood streamed down around them. As a guard blew his whistle, everyone had to go back to work. All the prisoners' faces were dismal.

I thought, *Is clay worth sacrificing human lives over? Are we human? Am I human?* I hated to admit that my life was so insignificant.

A few minutes later, a truck arrived to carry out the dead body. One chief guard commanded, "Take the living ones, too."

All three male prisoners were dumped into the truck, and it disappeared into the orchard. No one ever saw the two wounded prisoners again.

A Taste of the Outside World

All the prisoners desired to taste the world outside the prison cell. Anytime the prisoners who worked outside came back into the prison, they brought something for the people who couldn't go out. If they found nothing to bring back, they brought in green leaves just to show something from the outside world. That day, they sneaked clay into the prison for those who remained inside. That night, all the prisoners tasted clay.

But the tragedy of the three male prisoners was not the end of the turmoil for that day. After the female prisoners who worked outside returned to their cells, many began to cry because of stomachaches.

An officer came and said, "What's wrong with you today? Killing three men was not enough trouble for you? You decided to eat clay, so just shut up!"

All the prisoners who had eaten a lot of clay screamed in pain and rolled over on the floor until they died. That night, about twenty women died from eating too much clay. But I was safe because I didn't each that much.

That day, if someone would have asked me what my favorite food was, I probably would have said it was clay. Although the clay caused so many deaths, I have never forgotten the wonderful taste of it.

Chapter 12

THE DISCIPLINE DEPARTMENT

THE DISCIPLINE DEPARTMENT WAS FILLED with people who failed to conform to prison life. Their length of stay depended on how well they behaved there.

Prisoners in the discipline department were not allowed to meet with or write letters to their families. Often their prison sentences were extended. Ninety percent of the prisoners sent to the discipline department died before they ever got out of that place.

Prisoners who were sent to that department had the hardest and dirtiest job of all. They had to transfer human excrement to the farmland. When the prison toilets were full, these prisoners scooped out the contents with rubber baskets and poured it into a big tank. The feces tank was made of iron and weighed 800 kilograms (1,700 pounds). Usually, a team of five prisoners moved the tank on a cart.

The prison rules clearly said that prisoners were not allowed to talk more than was necessary. But whenever a newcomer joined a team, the other prisoners asked about the outside world. They wanted to know what changes had taken place and how people were living on the outside.

When an officer or guard discovered prisoners talking, he sent the prisoner to solitary confinement. But first the prisoner had to write a document criticizing her own behavior, then her fellow prisoners sat around her and had to criticize her, too. If a prisoner could not think of anything to say, she was also sent to solitary confinement. Prisoners who repeatedly broke the no-talking policy were sent to the discipline department.

Women Sent to the Discipline Department

Prisoners were sent to the discipline department for many reasons. One thirty-year-old woman was sent because she laughed. She was working at the shoe factory when she noticed the funny-looking shoe she had just made, so she laughed. An officer saw her breaking the rule, so he sent her to the discipline department.

Another woman was sent to the discipline department because she looked at her own reflection in a window. The warden saw her glancing at herself. He was hateful looking and had a hateful attitude. His fat body strutted around the prison and he looked at the prisoners like a poisonous snake would stare at its prey. Therefore, whenever he entered a factory, there was total silence except for the sound of machinery running. He would come in and say things like, "Hey, who feels that this is hard work? Who wants to die? I can help you with that!" I thought, *Killing people is one of his favorite hobbies.*

When he saw the woman glancing at herself in the mirror, he shouted, "Hey! Look at yourself! Do you want me to poke your eyeballs out?" Then he ordered her to go to the discipline department.

The favorite job of the prisoners in the discipline department was cleaning the pig sty. The prison pigs were fed a lot better than the prisoners because the officers wanted to fatten the pigs before they were butchered. While the prisoners cleaned, they devoured the pigs' leftovers with hands that had just worked in the toilet. Some of the prisoners envied the pigs. Someone said, "I wish I were a pig. Pigs eat a lot and sleep whenever they want."

One of the women who fed the pigs had a warm heart and a pretty face. She knew that the discipline department prisoners came to eat the pigs' leftovers so she always poured the thick corn soup into the pig stalls right before these prisoners arrived. Then the prisoners could enjoy "a delicious feast" with the pigs.

She continued feeding the pigs when she was alone with the prisoners. Her officer noticed it. She was dragged to the interrogation office and beaten until she was unconscious. No one ever saw her again after that.

In October 1989, about 230 female prisoners were secretly taken somewhere for a month. After they came back, I heard that they had gone to a concentration camp in Hwachen City to turn the political prison concentration camp into a rehabilitation camp for women.

This concentration camp had lots of cattle and crops. The female prisoners were given the job of butchering the cows, pigs, ducks, and chickens and shipping the meat and crops to the government. After butchering an animal, the prisoners had the privilege of eating its organs. The prisoners boiled the organs and shared them with each other.

The officers who took the female prisoners to the concentration camp were very busy sneaking out food such as corn, beans, oil, and meat. They made the female officers load all the food into their cars.

For some reason, the prisoners came back to Khechen prison after only a month. The officers wanted them to keep secret the fact that they had stolen food. But gossip about that spread around the prison. It was rumored that one officer took more than a ton of corn and beans.

The officers found out that the prisoners had gossiped about them. A few prisoners were sent to the discipline department and seven or eight women disappeared forever.

Five Died in the Feces Tank

When I first arrived in the prison, there were about twenty women who received ten-year sentences because they were classified as superstition believers. Every year their numbers increased. Many seemed to be about sixty or seventy years old. By 1992, there were between 100 and 120 believers. Instead of denying their faith, they worked harder in silence and patience. They were often kicked and beaten by the officers who wanted them to deny their faith. But not one of them denied; they all kept their faith.

Once a month, the believers were placed in the yard in front of all the prisoners and asked to deny their belief. The officers told them that if they did, they would receive a less difficult assignment in prison. Sometimes they even tried to persuade those prisoners by telling them they would be freed if they denied their faith. Since they would not deny their faith, they were given the most difficult work such as cleaning the toilets and removing the human excrement.

Because I thought they were merely superstitious, I decided they must not be very intelligent. I asked myself, "Why do they suffer so much by believing in a heaven that doesn't exist? All they have to say is that they no longer believe. They must be crazy." I hated them because they believed in a heaven I could not even see.

During the summer monsoon season of 1991, a team of six prisoners had to carry the ton of human excrement from the toilets to the large feces tank in the pouring rain. One day the prisoners couldn't open the door to the tank, so a woman named Ok Dan Lee climbed up on the tank to open it.

The tank was slippery because of the rain, so her feet slipped and she fell into the tank. As soon as the other prisoners saw her fall, they tried to rescue her. Because the tank was so deep, they needed a rope they could lower to help Ok Dan. Instead, one of her friends came to help her.

"Sister, can you come out?" she asked.

"I'm having a difficult time," Ok Dan answered.

"Let me come up and help."

An officer tried to stop her. "Do not go up there if you don't want to be like her. Just let her die!"

But the woman climbed up into the tank to help her friend Ok Dan out of the tank. But the tank was still too high. Then another woman jumped in and another. In all, four more women jumped into the tank to help their friends. Each of them tried to push the others up first.

Then the officer said, "Close the door." The door was closed and the women were left in the tank. Human manure is so poisonous that exposure to it will kill in a short time. No one ever tried to take the bodies out.

Later, I learned that the four who had jumped in to save Ok Dan were also Christians. They certainly expressed the love of their God.

I couldn't understand their actions because I didn't know their God then. Although they were not permitted to talk to each other, they would die for each other. If another prisoner did something wrong, a Christian would take responsibility and then was beaten until she died. When I saw their love, it raised questions in my mind that I could not erase. How could they die for someone else? What was there about heaven that was worth the cost of death?

Chapter 13

ALL FOR KIM IL SUNG

NORTH KOREA HAS A SHORTAGE OF electricity, so the government alternates the locations that are supplied power. Khechen Prison was supplied from the SongBae plant in South Pyong-An Province. For half the month, power came on only after 10 p.m. During the day when we had no power, the sewing machines had to be run manually.

The prisoners had to meet the production deadline regardless of how ill they were. The majority of the women were either sick or deformed. Yet the prisoners had to supply power by hand-spinning the main motor to which all one hundred sewing machines were connected.

A group of about ten female prisoners would take turns spinning the motor for one hour. The women were tiny, weak, and helpless. While they spun the belt, they easily became exhausted and their sweat dripped like rain. If one of the women stopped spinning, the sewing machines stopped as well. That caused inferior goods to be produced. Therefore, the officers stood in front of the woman spinning the motor and whipped her if she staggered even a little bit. Although the rehabilitation was supposed to be set up to change the thinking of the prisoners, it was actually used as sixteen to eighteen hours of free labor.

The hands of the prisoners who worked in the shoe factory had calluses all over them because they had to put the tiny nails into the shoes with their bare hands. Each pair of shoes took about 2,400 small nails, and each prisoner had to meet her quota of shoes every day to receive

Suddenly she drank the sewing machine chemicals—hydrochloric acid.

her daily allotment of 100 grams (3.5 ounces) of rice. If a prisoner couldn't meet her quota, she had to stay at the factory until she completed it. Everyone on her team had to wait for her to finish. Therefore, these prisoners lost their four to five hours of precious sleep.

In January 1992, a woman named Myung Sook Kim committed suicide in the shoe factory. She was a very skillful worker. Whenever the

1960 German-made sewing machine broke down—which was often—
her officers kicked her and urged her to finish the last step in making a
shoe. Since she had to produce the same number of shoes with or without the machine, the longer it took her to fix it, the more frustrated and
nervous she became. Suddenly, she grabbed the hydrochloric acid, which
was used to repair the sewing machine, and drank it.

Her body organs were eaten away by the acid, and she died in terrible pain. After she died, a special re-civilization training session was
given to all prisoners to criticize her suicide. Weekly training sessions
were changed to daily sessions. All three hundred prisoners who were
in the shoe factory had to stand for an hour criticizing each other.
Standing itself was difficult, but the sessions were conducted at midnight.

30,000 Birthday Presents

From January to April 1992, the prisoners slept only two hours a night
so they could complete Kim Il Sung's birthday presents by April 15. For
his 80th birthday, all students and workers were to receive a present.
Khechen Prison had to produce 10,000 student uniforms and 20,000
pieces of clothing for government workers in the public security bureaus,
rehabilitation camps, labor camps, and revolution managing departments. The presents had to be delivered by April 14.

The prisoners spent day and night in the factory. They worked, ate,
and slept at their positions. No one ever went back to the cell to sleep
on her back.

Since the prisoners were always drowsy, they often drove their hands
under the sewing machine needles. Although they were hurt or very
tired, they could never scream or take a rest because the officers would
beat them. When a prisoner injured herself, she just put sewing machine oil on her bleeding finger and went back to work.

No matter how well the prisoners did their jobs, if they made one
small mistake, the consequences were great. One inspector approved an
inferior piece of clothing because she was not wide awake while she was
working. Unfortunately, her mistake was discovered by her officer, and
she was sent to the discipline department.

Finally, the factory completed the 30,000 pieces of clothing on time.

Memorizing Kim Il Sung's Speech

Every New Year's Day, Kim Il Sung gave a speech to all North Koreans. The prisoners were required to memorize the speech word for word.

On the day Kim Il Sung gave the speech, the prisoners did not go into the factories. They sat in their cells and listened to the speech nine times. The team leader watched the prisoners and reported those who didn't pay attention to Kim Il Sung.

The next day, the speech was transcribed and a copy delivered to each team. The speech was long enough to fill two pages of a newspaper. It was a great challenge to memorize the speech word for word. However, the officers said that Kim Il Sung's speech was a remedy for the worries of families and complaints against the government.

The prisoners had to memorize the entire speech by April 15, Kim Il Sung's birthday. The prisoners always carried the manuscript with them and memorized it while they worked. Every night from 12:30 to 1:30 a.m., the officers checked to see how much of the speech the prisoners had memorized.

Surprisingly, 60 percent of the prisoners memorized it word for word. The elderly prisoners only had to memorize the content. But the younger prisoners who could not memorize the entire speech had their food ration cut.

The warden yelled at the prisoners, "Did you all memorize the speech? If you do not want to go to solitary confinement, you'd better hurry!" Whenever he came in and yelled at the prisoners, no one even breathed deeply.

When prisoners were called out once or twice a month to be criticized by other prisoners, some were criticized because they couldn't memorize the speech. Fifty-eight-year-old Jun Ji Jun, who worked in the export factory, had an especially hard time memorizing the speech. He used to be a farmer in Youngchen City in North Pyong-An Province. He was given a three-year prison sentence because he sold seashells to Chinese people to pay for his son's wedding. Selling a seashell is considered an illegal export activity.

He was having a hard time memorizing the speech, so he was beaten and given less food. Because of this, he suffered from a hernia and malnutrition. When an officer made him recite the speech, his mind went blank. He was placed in solitary confinement. A few days after his release, he died while working at the factory. His body turned cold, so everyone knew he was dead.

The warden ordered fifty-year-old Ok Sun Kim to recite the speech. She stood up and her body shivered. She was frozen with fear and couldn't speak.

The warden commanded, "Put her in solitary confinement!"

She was immediately dragged to solitary confinement. After she was released, her legs were paralyzed and she suffered from a hernia. The officers noticed her body deteriorating and they bluntly said, "Let her die." She died without any medical treatment.

Hung Bum Kim was also in her fifties. She was an ordinary farmer and could not read. Therefore, she couldn't memorize the speech.

Although she was always skillful at her manual work, her lack of education caused her to receive smaller food rations for a month. To fill her empty stomach, she drank the water used to clean the toilets.

After she was sent to solitary confinement, she was also paralyzed. However, she was still put to work in the factory. One cold day as the wind came through a broken window, someone discovered her dead body under a pile of fabric.

One man used to be a director in the Central Bank in Pyongyang City. When the warden pointed to him and commanded him to recite Kim Il Sung's speech, he cried, "I can die, but I cannot memorize the speech!"

His lamentation was considered an insult to Kim Il Sung and he was executed publicly.

Re-education Training Session

Wherever there was a re-education training session, the prisoners worked even harder because they still had to complete their quota even though they were forced to quit working early. During the July 1989 training session, the prisoners were required to listen to a radio program. It was about Su Kyung Im who was part of a radical movement in South Korea where she was born. She was a university student who had a fervent desire to unify North and South Korea. She illegally left the South and came to North Korea.

The radio speaker praised Su Kyung Im as the hope for Communist unification of the two Koreas, and referred to her as the daughter of Kim Il Sung and the daughter of Korea. She wanted to return to South Korea through Panmunjum, the landmark that divides the North and the

He cried, "I can die, but I cannot memorize the speech!"

South. When the North allowed her to return to South Korea through Panmunjum, she was arrested by the South. The speaker said that the North Korean government should protest Sun Kyung Im's arrest to the International Human Rights Committee. The speaker also said that North Korean journalists who visited South Korea sent many presents to Su Kyung Im's parents.

I wondered why the South Korean government did not execute Su Kyung Im. Would North Korea have let her live after she visited South Korea illegally?

I compared the treatment of prisoners between North and South

Korea, and realized that the South treated criminals differently than the North. In North Korea, she and her family would have been destroyed immediately. From that time on, I began to doubt my former beliefs about South Korea. At least South Korea had respect for human rights and freedom.

Later, I learned that Sun Kyung Im had confessed her crime and the government set her free. After I was released from prison, that radio program encouraged me to defect to South Korea where people are treated like people.

Chapter 14

THE PEOPLE WHO BELIEVED IN GOD

ALL MY LIFE, I HAD BEEN TAUGHT THAT religion was like a drug. I learned in school that religion paralyzes human creativity and logic. I was well-trained to never think about God's existence.

Having Christians in a nation that believes Kim Il Sung as a god violates a fundamental belief. Because of this belief among North Korean leaders, oppression against Christians in North Korea is especially severe. Since the North Korean government was established, the leaders have tried to eliminate all religions through intense persecution. People who will not deny their faith in God are sent to concentration camps or prisons. I believed that it was their choice to live as worthless animals instead of as a traitor to God. Yet, there was a spark in me that wanted to know God. When I was in prison, I would look up in the sky and cry out, "Why are you doing this to me?"

I couldn't understand these believers who were aware of an "invisible power." The abuse they received was so much greater than the abuse other prisoners got. If a prison guard finds a way to convince a person to deny God, the guard will get promoted. So the guards try any way possible to do this. The believers received less food and clothing rations, and were isolated from the other prisoners.

In some instances while believers were being beaten, they would stand up halfway and begin to sing hymns and say "Amen." The guards thought they were crazy and took them back to the electric torture room. I never saw any of the believers return from that room. I, too, thought they were crazy, and I didn't understand what they were singing.

Yet the believers didn't become evil after the abuse they received. If a prisoner made a mistake, she had to pay severe consequences. Therefore, some prisoners blamed their mistakes on other prisoners. But the Christian group was different. They not only did not falsely accuse others, but were willing to take the blame for another. They even died for other prisoners.

Just like the believers who worked in the discipline department, other believers were given the most horrible jobs in prison. When I first entered a prison factory, I saw people working on the rubber soles of shoes. They wore only rubber aprons and were covered with black rubber powder. The only thing I could see beyond the black powder was their white teeth shining from their dark faces.

Later, I found out that these prisoners were the people of God. They were given the most dangerous work in the prison. The rubber factory, smelting factory, mine, and discipline department were the main places they were assigned.

Of all these places, the rubber factory was the worst. After the rubber was heated, it went under a big roller to be flattened. The prisoners' job was to flip over the hot rubber before it went under the roller. Officers forced the believers to do this work to "re-civilize" them. The rubber was very heavy, and if the prisoners didn't flip it fast enough, their hands and arms were smashed by the roller. Many of these prisoners had lost hands and arms.

Working in the Rubber Factory

In July 1991, all the prisoners were working more than twenty hours every day to finish the extra projects for Kim Il Sung's 80th birthday on April 15, 1992. Working twenty hours in the rubber factory squeezed every drop of human strength out of the prisoners. Yet the officers pestered the prisoners, calling them lazy and accusing them of trying to sabotage the project.

One Christian man always worked quietly at his job of flipping the rubber. One day, his fatigued body stumbled onto the hot rubber and he began to get sucked into the roller.

A prisoner screamed at an officer, "Someone is dying! Turn off the roller!"

The officer yelled back, "Don't stop the machine! It's our chance to remove this crazy, godly man!"

I realized once again that the officers didn't have a conscience. They were like Satan—getting their thrills by watching the pain of prisoners.

One spring day in 1992, the rubber factory burned to the ground. Because the factory stored a lot of gasoline, the fire roared up and engulfed the whole building almost instantly. One of the main factory buildings was located right next to the rubber factory. The fire truck soaked the factory with water, but the water didn't even faze the fire.

There were twenty to thirty prisoners trapped inside the rubber factory, waiting to be saved. It was possible to rescue the prisoners and protect the adjacent building at the same time, but the warden came and decided to shut the rubber factory door to protect the building. He considered the prisoners too worthless to take any time for them in that emergency situation.

Walking on Bodies

Once or twice a month, on a Sunday or Saturday, the guards would pull out one or two Christians for re-education training. (They used many harsh words like "fight to gain the correct Communist philosophy or mind.") The six thousand other prisoners would surround the Christians as the guards tried to get the believers to deny heaven.

One day, the warden pulled out one of the men. The guards hung the believer upside down. The warden screamed, "Say that you don't believe in heaven! Heaven is only a word. Just say, 'I don't believe in heaven.'"

The believer didn't say a word, either yes or no. The warden began to poke him with a stick until his whole body was bloody. Then he was let down and the warden kicked and beat him. But still he did not deny his faith.

The warden was furious. He looked like he had been taking drugs to make him high. He began to stomp on the Christian, reminding the other prisoners, "This is going to happen to you if you ever believe in heaven!"

Then the warden ordered all the prisoners to walk over the body of the Christian. It was totally unimaginable how he died.

Another time, two men were pulled out and ordered to deny heaven. (The word "god" was never allowed to be spoken.) But the men would not deny their religion.

Again, all six thousand prisoners were ordered to walk over their bodies. Just think of six thousand people walking over them! For the first two or three minutes, the men screamed with a very strange sound. The screams sounded like the cry of dogs as they are hung with ropes. Yet the believers never said any words other than "the Lord...the Lord." I did not know why they were calling the Lord. But I know they were expressing their conviction in the Lord.

The Smelting Factory

One night in February 1992, I went to the smelting factory. The work was almost done for the day and I had to check the daily production.

I saw eight Christian prisoners carrying a big metal kettle holding molten iron. An officer called to them using very vile words. "Tomorrow is the day of re-education training. As you know, it's held because of your stubbornness. You are supposed to turn yourself in. Tomorrow is a 'cleaning the mind' day. Tomorrow, you will go out and tell everyone that there is nothing in heaven to believe in; there is no God. Otherwise you will be killed. Do you understand?"

There was silence. Not one of the prisoners responded to the officer. He didn't wait long for an answer because he didn't like to be ignored. He knew that tomorrow was an important day for re-education and he wanted the believers to recant. He yelled at the prisoners, "Why are you so quiet? Answer me! Answer me now!"

No one said a word.

The officer became furious and began to curse at the men. At the top of his voice, he screamed, "You sons of b——es! All eight of you come here and put your face down to the ground!"

They came just as he ordered. They sat on their knees and then bent their heads down.

The officer called over other male prisoners, "We cannot let these men live. They think they don't know who I am. Bring boiling liquid iron from the furnace and pour it on them!"

The male prisoners' faces were full of fear. The liquid iron was 1,200 degrees. They hesitated to do this terrible thing.

The officer gave them a fierce scowl. "Do you want to die with them?"

This painting at a North Korean museum depicts conditions in the smelting factory, where prisoners worked with liquid iron at 1,200 degrees.

They poured boiling metal on top of the people of God.

The frightened prisoners ran to get a kettle of molten iron. Then they poured the boiling iron on top of the people of God kneeling so quietly.

Suddenly, the smell of burning flesh assailed my nostrils. The bodies began to shrivel from the intense heat as the liquid metal burned right through their flesh.

I fell to the ground and almost fainted from shock. The impact on me was so tremendous that I screamed as if I were crazy. Other prisoners in the factory screamed in horror as the eight Christians died.

I looked at their shrunken bodies and wondered in my heart, *What do they believe? What do they see in the empty sky? What could be more important to them than their lives?*

In the years I was in prison, I saw many believers die. Yet they never, never denied the God who is in heaven. All they had to do was say they don't believe in religion and they would have been released.

I didn't understand what made them not fear death. Their unbelievable faith brought a big question into my heart: *What did they see, and what am I missing?*

Chapter 15

THE SON WHO LIVED IN AMERICA

MY PRISON EXPERIENCE COMPLETELY destroyed my belief in communism and all the things I had been taught. I couldn't understand why the government treated people so unfairly and why the officers had no regard for the prisoners. Many of these hard-working, abused people had not done anything to deserve the punishment they received.

Sometimes people see the truth. That happened to me. I saw some of the absurdity of the North Korean government before I was sent to prison, but my childhood training in Kim Il Sung's doctrine kept me from seeing the truth. It wasn't until I suffered from the injustice that I began to change my mind. Then my eyes were opened to the system I was living in.

I recalled an incident that happened when I was still happily working as an accountant in the commercial department of Onsung County. I lived in one of the nicer houses because of my position. One morning as I arrived at work, my boss summoned me to his office. I knocked on his door, thinking, *It's very early for a meeting.*

My boss enthusiastically welcomed me and apologized for calling me so early in the morning. Suddenly, he lowered his voice. "We want to ask you for help. And I believe that you are willing to help us."

He began to explain the situation. "There is an old lady from our town who has a son who lives in America. Her son applied to the government to visit his family. However, the old lady doesn't have a house so we want to pretend that your house is her house. Giving a good impression to the man from America is important to protect the honor of Kim Il Sung. We have to make this American believe that his mother is living happily in a nice house."

Because my boss said that he was just trying to protect the honor of Kim Il Sung, I couldn't refuse his request. He said, "Take the day off and go back to your house. The family will be waiting for you at home."

At that moment, I understood that I didn't have the option of saying no. Everything had already been planned before my boss even asked me.

An Old Friend

When I arrived at home and saw the family who would occupy my house, I recognized familiar faces I hadn't seen in a long time. I knew the old lady and her daughter, who was my good friend Mi Hee Choi.

During the Korean War, my parents had moved to another town called Sesun to take refuge. At that time, I attended school with Mi Hee. We used to play hide-and-seek together. Later, we went to different colleges and lost track of each other. Mi Hee's mother moved to Pyongyang City with her youngest son. Mi Hee became a teacher, and her husband was an inspector in a customs house.

When Mi Hee's mother found out that it was my home she was to occupy, she sighed. "I'm sorry for taking your house. But I am glad this is your house." Because she knew she was going to see her son soon, her face gleamed.

Soon after I brought them into my home, the government officials came to check on whether my house was good enough to bring in an important guest. They complimented me by saying that my house was even better than the houses of high officials.

After the officers left, I was alone with the two women. I asked them for more details on why they were moving into my house.

Mi Hee's mother began to cry as she explained her story. She had two sons and two daughters. When the oldest son, Il Sung Choi, was eighteen years old, the Korean War broke out and he joined the army. During the war, he was captured by the South Korean army and never returned home. At one time, North and South Korean prisoners of war were exchanged, but since Il Sung Choi wasn't among them, everyone thought he was dead. As a result, his family was treated like a war hero's family. The government allowed Il Sung Choi's sisters and brother to get a good education and jobs. The daughters married successful men, and the youngest son was promoted to a position in Pyongyang City.

But everything changed when the government learned that the oldest son everyone thought was dead was instead living in America. They found this out when he asked the North Korean government to permit him to visit his family.

At that moment, Il Sung Choi's family went from being considered the family of a war hero to the family of a traitor. He lived in America —the enemy of North Korea. The younger son was demoted to a local buyer, and his family had to move into a storage building. The mother's grief for her younger son squelched the joy she felt in meeting her oldest son who she had once thought was dead.

The mother sighed deeply. "My son is coming home alive. I thought he was dead. I miss him so much. But I would have been happier if I had never found out that he was alive. Son, why do you want to see me after all these years and cause all these problems?"

The Visit

Mi Hee's mother was going to take her six-year-old granddaughter to Pyongyang City to meet her oldest son. The little girl had been trained to tell the son about how much Kim Il Sung had blessed the family. The little girl repeated the words like a parrot. "My father is Kim Il Sung. My mother is the government." The little girl even recited the words while she was sleeping.

Days before Il Sung Choi came, there was a big fuss in town. Every home in my neighborhood had received their half-month food ration early so they could pretend that North Korea has plenty of food. Before he arrived, everyone was called out to clean and repair the street. The government commanded that no one could come close to my house while Il Sung Choi's family was staying there. My husband and I had been moved out to a security office.

Finally, the day came for the son's arrival. The mother went to the airport to meet the son who had left her house about thirty-five years ago. When she saw her son, he no longer looked like she remembered him.

He had gray hair and wrinkles on his face.

Her son bowed before her and cried as he greeted his mother. "Mother! Your son has finally come to see you!"

Mother and son held each other for a long time and cried. Then some officers took them to Kim Il Sung's statute and told him to pray for the great leader's long life. But he stood there and didn't say anything.

His behavior was reported to the government.

Then Il Sung Choi and his mother came to my house. He wanted to meet some of his old friends, but none of them showed up. He was not allowed to go to certain places that were not clean or well-developed. Mi Hee and her husband also stayed in my house. Mi Hee's family didn't know how to use all the electrical appliances because they had never seen them before. They didn't know how to control the color on the television set and they put fresh vegetables in the freezer.

Finally, Il Sung Choi asked, "Whose house is this?"

Mi Hee answered, "Of course, it's mother's house." However, she thought that he noticed something was wrong.

Many government officials stayed with the family to listen to their every conversation and watch their actions. They never let the mother and son spend time alone. Government officials even slept in the same room.

The son had to leave many days later. He gave some U.S. dollars to his mother and sister. Mi Hee's mother wailed in front of me after her son left. The government officials confiscated the money her son had given them.

The Consequences of a Son's Visit

My friend Mi Hee's life was totally destroyed by her brother's appearance. His behavior was deemed anti-Communist by the government. At a meeting in the Public Security Bureau, one man stood up and criticized Il Sung Choi's behavior. He said that people like him will advertise only the bad things about North Korea. They will take only bad pictures to show to people back home.

Mi Hee's husband asked her for a divorce. He said that he couldn't live with a woman whose brother is a traitorous American citizen. She was so devastated about losing her family that she ended up in a mental hospital. Mi Hee's cousin also got a divorce for the same reason.

Now that I had seen in prison how the government really works, how greedy and selfish government officials are, I understood more about Il Sung Choi's family's problems. I thought, *When a person who was thought dead comes back alive, people should be joyful. But Il Sung Choi's visit only brought great disappointment and grief.* This is the sad plight of the North Korean people.

Chapter 16

SHADOW OF THE COMMUNIST PARADISE

PRISONERS WERE NOT THE ONLY sufferers in North Korea. Once my eyes were opened to the truth about the Communist government and Kim Il Sung's policies, I began to realize how difficult the lives of the North Korean people were. What was supposed to be a Communist paradise was actually a place of oppression and cruelty.

North Koreans are manipulated by their government. The people believe all the lies the government tells them. In the summer of 1989, the national security department sent out an announcement stating that every person who had heard a foreign broadcast or saw a foreign news pamphlet, especially those from South Korea, had to confess. The announcement also said that those who confessed would be forgiven.

The day the announcement came out in the prison, some prisoners confessed. They all disappeared instead of being forgiven. The result of the North Koreans' faith was always death.

The Plight of Foreigners
Many of the foreign people in North Korea had sad life stories. Right after the Korean War, the North Korean government advertised itself as a nation of paradise. They wanted to attract foreigners and Koreans who

lived in the Third World to move to North Korea. Many people came to North Korea because of those advertisements.

A Chinese woman moved to North Korea with her husband. After he was arrested by a national security soldier, she searched for him and finally got an answer from a soldier. He informed her, "Your husband was not faithful to the government; therefore, he will not return to his family."

Many Japanese people also moved to North Korea. A few had relatives who sent them money from Japan so they could live better lives. But most of them had to sell everything they had little by little until they became poor. As foreigners, they didn't receive any benefits from the government. The foreign women often lived by conducting small businesses, which were banned by the government, and then were arrested for doing black marketing.

In Khechen Prison alone, there were about 250 Korean-Japanese women. One Japanese woman became mentally ill after she watched a public execution. She was killed by "electric treatment," which is actually torture.

In the fall of 1989, all the Japanese prisoners were released to celebrate the 30th anniversary of the immigration program. But many of them were just arrested again and sent back to prison right after their release.

Two Japanese women came to North Korea with their husbands. The husbands became seriously ill and died at a young age. These foreign women were forced to sustain their families by running small businesses. Eventually, they too were arrested and sent to prison.

I think about one woman from my hometown who had a sad life. She was a Japanese lady in her fifties who came with her Korean husband, Gi Il Kim, who was in his sixties. He was a driver who distributed food. He had married her in Japan and then moved back to North Korea in the 1960s. The government commanded him to bring back the rest of his family, so his wife came to North Korea with their two children. They left their oldest son in Japan.

When she moved to North Korea, she brought two Toyota passenger cars, a truck, and many electrical appliances. But the government forced the couple to contribute almost everything she had brought to the government. The Public Security Bureau officers would say they were "borrowing" the items, but they were never returned.

When this woman first came to North Korea, her skin was very fair.

People in the street always took a second look at her clothing and face. But she was having a hard time adjusting to the poorer life she now had to live. To obtain food, she had to barter her watch and clothes. When the family first arrived, the government began to watch Gi Il Kim; they thought he might be a spy simply because he had a Japanese wife. The family originally lived in a nice apartment, but the government moved them to a rural area because their apartment was located on a street where Kim Il Sung and Kim Jong Il passed by.

This couple had a son who attended my husband's school. The son was very intelligent and talented in soccer. One time, the national soccer team scouts came to recruit him, but he could not join them because he had a Japanese mother.

Over the years, the Japanese lady's beauty faded away. Her face began to show signs of suffering in North Korea. She looked very old. She no longer had any assets to maintain a decent life nor anyone from Japan to send her money to help her live. She missed her brothers and sisters, and until the day she died, her wish was to meet them.

A man named Chung Ha Kim had a wealthy uncle in Japan. His uncle believed in democracy and supported South Korea. The North Korean government sent Chung Ha Kim to Japan on a mission to persuade his uncle to support North Korea. When he met his uncle publicly, he praised North Korea. As soon as they were alone, he secretly told his uncle all about the problems in North Korea. When Chung Ha Kim came back to North Korea, the government learned of his betrayal. He was killed in October 1987.

The South Korea War Prisoners

When I worked in the commercial department, I knew a few South Korean war prisoners. They had been captured during the Korean Conflict. After the war, hundreds of them were imprisoned in a concentration camp. In 1971, they were scattered to work in many different mines. At that time, my job included delivering goods to these people.

The South Korean war prisoners were treated like forced labor slaves. They lived in isolation and were restricted from working with North Korean citizens. The South Koreans lived in poverty. At home, they didn't even have enough blankets to cover their bodies. They were not given equipment to do their work so they had to shovel and dig in the most primitive ways. Many spent all their lives in the mine.

The South Koreans were allowed to marry only women from lower class families. Their children's education was limited to middle school and they were not allowed to join the army. Their sons' futures were working in the mine with their fathers.

Once I had the opportunity to go into a mine. The cave was less than one meter (3 feet) high, so all the men worked on their knees with shovels and hoes. I asked my coworker who these men were, and he told me they were South Korean war prisoners.

I remember a few of the South Korean war prisoners I had met. Kyung Jo Kim was from Kyungsang Province. He used to be a farmer and had a wife and two children. When the Korean Conflict broke out, he lied to his wife. He told her he was going to the city for a month to find a better job. He thought that the war would be over in a month.

His wife anxiously asked him, "Are you sure you're not joining the army?"

The day he left home, his wife handed him a rice cake wrapped in linen. He always carried the linen cloth in his clothes. But he lost both the linen and one leg when he was tortured in a North Korean concentration camp.

A man named Jong Un Kim from Chungchun Province left behind his wife to join the army just a few months after their wedding. The last letter he received from her said that she was expecting his first child.

He missed his beautiful wife. He said, "I know that my wife is holding her bridal shoes to her breast, waiting for me to come back."

He loved to tell stories about his wife. They had grown up in the same town. Often, he would hide in a tree and call to her to find him. If she could not find him, he dropped a persimmon to her.

Someone asked him, "You have a wife here. Yet you are always talking about the wife in South Korea. After the unification of South and North Korea, what are you going to tell your North Korean wife? Are you going to abandon her?"

He answered, "My wife here is temporary. My South Korean wife is my only wife. I'm going to her as soon as the nation is unified."

Someone teased him, "Do you really believe that your wife is still waiting for you? I'll bet that she has already found a good man and remarried."

He answered with a firm, stern voice, "No way! I know her. She will always wait for me."

Jong Un Kim had a beautiful singing voice. When he sang the folk songs he had learned in South Korea, he made people cry.

All the war prisoners had the same hope. They wanted to return to their homeland after the reunification. One phenomenon that I thought was very strange was that although they worked in the most dangerous places, their mines never collapsed. On the other hand, other mines caved in despite all the precautions taken. Perhaps God gave extra protection to the poor South Koreans who lived with sad hearts.

Truly a dark shadow lays over the oppressed people of North Korea, a land that is described as a paradise by the Communist government.

Chapter 17

THE REAL ROBBERS IN PRISON

WHILE I WAS THE CHIEF ACCOUNTANT at Khechen Prison, I was put in charge of many jobs, such as calculating how much material to buy, planning quotas for each factory prisoner, and collecting statistics. Since my job was so broad, I had many bosses. They included a financial officer, a labor officer, a planning officer, and a production officer. They were all young men who had just graduated from business college. They had no business experience or practical knowledge. I actually did all their work.

My life wasn't any easier than any of the other prisoners except that I was allowed to take a shower whenever I wanted to and I wore a clean uniform. These privileges were not for my comfort, but because the officers didn't want to share the office with a smelly prisoner. All the other prisoners smelled really bad because they could never wash themselves. When the officers came into the factory, they couldn't stand the smell so they covered their noses with their handkerchiefs.

Soon I became a person who could make a big difference to the prison officials. The government gave the prison a certain amount of fabric to make a certain number of goods. If I strictly followed the government's instructions on how to lay out the patterns, there would be piles of scraps left after the patterns were cut out. Depending on how I laid the pattern, I could save a lot of fabric. If I arranged everything well, the prison saved hundreds of meters of fabric and leather every year. I ended up with stocks of leftovers. But they were not mine. They didn't belong to anyone.

Actually, all the leftovers went into the pockets of the officers. They came to me and asked for leftovers. Through me, they took fabric, shoes, bags, belts, and everything else made in the factories. I often thought, *If all the saved material was distributed to poor people, their lives would be a lot easier.*

Whenever the officers asked me for leftovers, I had to obey them since I was a prisoner. Therefore, the officers didn't abuse me as they did the other prisoners.

Even the warden was involved in the stealing. He came to me and said, "My son needs some fabric to make an army uniform." He took what he wanted without letting the assistant warden know what was going on.

The officers put a lot of trust in me because I never broke prison policy. But I always had an uneasy feeling about getting involved in so much underground activity. I had heard people say that knowing too many secrets brings an early death. Since the leftover material wasn't recorded anywhere, I made my own secret account book, recording what the officers had stolen. I spared my own life by keeping everything I knew a secret. I never told anyone which officers took what or how much.

The Greedy Officers

One time, the financial officer ordered me to make 8,000 pairs of gloves with leftover leather and nylon. As soon as the gloves were completed, the other officers came and took them. By the time the financial officer came to get his order, everything was gone. He scolded me for giving the gloves away to the other officers because he was going to use them as bribes for higher officials. But he couldn't punish me because his activities were illegal.

In the fall when the Koreans make *kim chi*, Korean cabbage pickles, the officers demanded a lot of quilted cotton shoes. They bartered the shoes for pickle ingredients such as garlic and pepper.

One lieutenant was looking toward her retirement. She came to me and took about 100 meters of Russian fabric as well as some thread. One officer sneaked 120 kilograms of pure cotton. One export officer took high-quality sweaters and gloves. Some took ten bags; some took fifty pairs of shoes.

I laughed secretly about the hypocritical behavior of the officers who took the leftovers for themselves. They were the real robbers. The real prisoners were innocent. However, the real robbers called the innocent people criminals. The officers sucked the sweat and blood of innocent people to fill their own stomachs and pockets.

Chapter 18

The Traitor Who Walked Out of Prison

ONE DAY, THE EMERGENCY BELL RANG, which usually signified a public execution of a prisoner. I ran outside wondering who would be executed this time.

When everyone had gathered, an officer stood up and called a name. The name was identical to mine! Yet I was the only one in the prison who had that name. My heart dropped. I couldn't understand what I had done wrong to deserve a public execution.

Two soldiers led me in front of everyone. The dreadful silence was broken by another officer's announcement. "Soon Ok Lee has faithfully worked for Kim Il Sung, so we decided to reward her work. She will be returned to society. I am telling all of you: If you work as hard as she did, you can also go back home."

At the moment the officer announced my release before the prisoners, the eyes of all six thousand prisoners—the tailless animals—stared at me. Even 140 Christians in the front row suddenly lifted their heads and looked at me. This was against prison policy. Kim Il Sung had ordered that Christians in the prison were never to be allowed to lift their heads and look up to the sky. These prisoners had seen only dirt since the time they had entered the black iron gates of the prison. Never had they been granted the privilege of seeing the blue sky—all because they believed in heaven. Yet, the moment the announcement was made, it was as if they had all agreed to do one last thing. They all looked up at me at once. Their eyes were glowing with a heavenly light. I knew their eyes were telling me, "When you get out of prison, be a witness for us. You are not going out just to live a better life. You are going out to tell about the real hell that exists in here." They were begging me to tell about their faith and witness about all that they were suffering. That is what their eyes reflected to me. I can never forget the sight of those pleading eyes.

Final Indoctrination

Whenever a prisoner finished her sentence, she was sent to the "expired prisoner's cell." This cell was designed to reinforce the soon-to-be-released prisoner's faith in Kim Il Sung and his doctrine. In order to be released from prison, the prisoner had to say, "While I was in prison, I strengthened my faith in Kim Il Sung. I learned a good lesson while I was in prison." Then the prisoner had to sign an oath stating, "If I divulge secrets about the prison, I will return to prison."

The prisoners were told that there were a few things they should not do once they left prison. They should never complain about anything regarding the prison nor take favors from other prisoners. They should say, "After I get out of prison, I will devote myself to Kim Il Sung until my death."

Usually lower level officers indoctrinated these prisoners, but in my case, the warden talked to me five times. He was afraid that I might speak out against his illegal deeds after I was released from prison. He came every few days and tried to talk to me. He admitted embezzling, but he justified that the leftovers had to go somewhere. Why not to him?

The warden informed me, "This is the first time since this prison was established that we are releasing a model prisoner. You brought so much benefit to the government. I will send a letter to your hometown officer about how well you have been re-educated. I hope you work as hard in society as you did here. The real worker stays faithful to the government until death."

A mother and a daughter shared a cell with me at one time during my indoctrination. They had been in prison for three years for stealing a corn bag. Fortunately, they had stayed alive until the day that their sentence expired. They were so happy to be done with prison life. But when the mother was about to leave the prison to return home to her husband, she discovered that he had divorced her while she was in prison.

In North Korea, when wives went to prison, their husbands were sent to a rural area far from the city or demoted unless they divorced their wives. Therefore, almost 90 percent of the female prisoners were divorced by their husbands. For that reason, most female prisoners didn't have a place to go to after they left prison. If they were released, they were sent back to their hometowns. They were usually assigned to work in construction sites or mines. Their weak bodies suffered from such heavy labor. I heard that released prisoners usually didn't live very long.

With downcast faces, the mother and her daughter came back with the officer. They told me that they were being sent to the Communist rehabilitation camp for the rest of their lives. I felt very sad for them.

My Release Day

On December 23, 1992, the warden called me out and again made me sit on my knees on the cold cement floor with my head bowed. My heart was filled with anger, but I had to be patient because my misery was almost over.

The warden asked me, "Do you want to tell me something before you go?"

I made up the best lie I could. I answered, "I am completely civilized with love for Kim Il Sung. I will never commit a crime again. Everything I experienced in prison will go to my grave with my body." But in my heart, I was thinking, *I was totally deceived by this nation. I am not staying here. I will run away.*

My lie satisfied the warden. He laughed with his sagging jowl flapping from side to side. He sauntered in a stately manner.

I looked at him with derision in my mind. I said, "Sir, I want to tell you one thing."

He looked at me and waited for me to speak.

I said calmly, "You keep telling me that I brought great benefit to the government. But where did all that benefit go? I know that it did not go back to the government nor to the needy people. I put all my efforts into saving more material. I wish that the materials had been used for the poor people and children instead."

I saw my son running toward me.

I had lived faithfully to serve the Party before and did so even now. I continued, "I will keep the secret of this place even to the day of my death. I am just asking you to use the leftovers for the poor people."

The warden's face became serious. He nodded as if he agreed with me. I didn't believe for a moment that he had sincerely adopted my advice. I thought, *He's just pretending to listen to my advice so that I will feel better.*

"Number 832, out!" someone yelled.

It was the moment I had dreamed about. I ran out of the prison with unbelievable joy. My legs were shaking and my heart was pumping so fast. I wasn't sure that this was not just a dream. It was too wonderful to be true!

I finally passed the iron gate that I had tried to run away from so many years ago. I was finally out of hell. It was a miracle!

I saw my son running toward me. My son cried, "Now everything is fine with life once again! Once again…"

The warden and several officers stood in front of the gate to see me off. This was the first time that prison officers came to see a prisoner leaving. They must have considered me a very special person since I had once been a high officer in the Party and was an innocent victim. But their greatest motivation for being nice to me was their fear that I might report their illegal activities.

One officer told my son, "Your mother must be happy to have a big son like you. Take care of your mother. She worked very hard."

The warden gave me some parting words. He said, "You are very lucky compared to other prisoners because you have a family to pick you up. From now on, stay faithful to the government, and take care of yourself!"

I will always remember his words, "You are very lucky."

In that resocialization prison, there were six thousand prisoners. In all of North Korea, there were probably two hundred thousand prisoners. I was one of the very few who got out. I was the first one in thirty years who was given the special privilege of a release from Kim Il Sung. No one else got out of prison before their sentence was completed.

Although I didn't know it at the time, this was surely the grace of God. I hadn't been any smarter than anyone else. God pulled me out of the real-world hell.

The Eyes of the Tailless Animals

The day was cold and the sky was so clear. I felt like the sky was celebrating my release.

As soon as my son and I were alone, I gripped his hand. I told him, "I can't live in this nation any longer. We have to go to another country."

My son was surprised by my harsh remark. He became furious. He said, "How dare you? I understand that you are upset, but you should be thankful to our father, Kim Il Sung, who let you out early! Don't ever say that again!"

Soon he softened his voice and told me, "Now we are free. The government can help us gain what we lost. I am sure that the Party will listen to us."

I looked at my son. I knew he couldn't understand me. No one could understand unless he experienced prison life like I had. I could never forget my six years in prison. I was released as a model prisoner, but I was actually a traitor to the nation. I was ready to run away. The only feeling I had toward North Korea was anger. This anger had sustained me while I was in their "hell."

Although I was happy to get out of prison, my mind was bothered by many thoughts. I remembered the moment when the officer announced my release before six thousand prisoners. The eyes of all six thousand prisoners—the tailless animals—stared at me. I couldn't forget their eyes. Every night, the eyes visited me in my dreams, wailing at me. I cried with them until my son woke me up. I panted while my son wiped the cold perspiration off my forehead.

The horror of prison life was a top secret in the North Korea. No one is allowed to talk about it, not even prison officers. If a person talks, he must die in prison. But God brought me out of that hell to use me to proclaim the tragedy of those who live in that horror. I continually pray for the reunification of Korea and that God will protect the prisoners until that day.

I am disgusted by the lies of the North Korean government. I once truly believed that North Korea was the paradise of the universe, but it is really the den of evil. Everyone in the world will see the reality of hell when the North Korean government is torn down.

Chapter 19

CROSSING THE TUMEN RIVER

I HAD LIVED IN NORTH KOREA WITHOUT knowing the truth. I had given my utmost loyalty to the Party and to Kim Il Sung and Kim Jong Il. I strived to do my best to work hard for the Party. The result of all my sincere, hard work and respect for the government was to spend time in prison. Whenever I remembered the many times I got excited about doing something for Kim Il Sung, I became very mad. I had trusted and loved a nation of falsehood which taught me to give up being human.

It had been six years from the morning I was dragged to the interrogation center to the day I walked out of prison. I had thoroughly experienced the true face of my country. For the first year in prison, I didn't understand why all these things were happening to me. Over the next five years, I really came to understand what the prison warden said about not being a human.

I used to believe that the North Korean government valued every individual. Then I found out that the government purposely allocated the number of people to be sent to prison so they could have free labor.

Every ten years, the government released many prisoners to celebrate Kim Il Sung's birthday, but I discovered that as soon as they were released, the government arrested more healthy people who could work more effectively. People who were released from prison received a new identification card showing that they were once criminals. Therefore, they were always watched. Many were returned to prison.

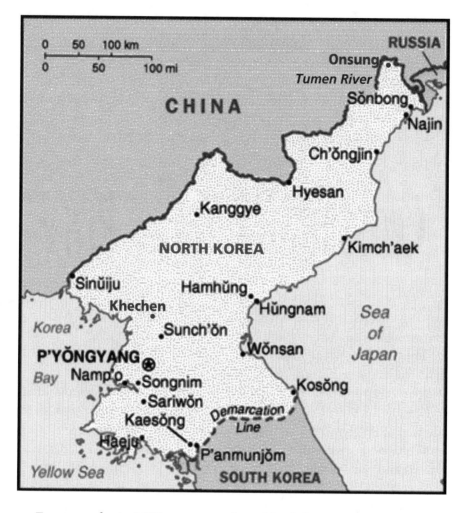

For example, in 1992, a woman from North Pyong-An Province was released to celebrate Kim Il Sung's birthday. When she got back home and saw her starving children, she snuck into a cornfield to gather some food. She was caught by a policeman and sent back to prison.

More Lies From the Government

When I left the prison, they sent me to a place that was used to retrain those who have been in jail. As I arrived at my old home in Onsung, I discovered that it was not the place I used to live. While I was gone, my son had been kicked out of the university and my husband had been dismissed from his principal's position and demoted to a farm worker. All my property, including my electrical appliances, valuable goods, and even clothes and shoes, had been confiscated. Judge Moon Kyu Park took my color television set; the public prosecutor took my refrigerator; a juror took my washing machine; and others took whatever they could grab in my house. All my personal jewelry disappeared. Someone even took my husband's jackets, shoes, and socks.

Worse yet, I didn't know where my husband was. When my son, Dong Chel, came back from the university, his father had disappeared. The government had taken him and they wouldn't tell us where he was. My family was living in such miserable conditions.

I remembered that the interrogation officer so many years ago had promised me that he would protect my family. My heart exploded in anger. This too had been a lie. I wrote letters of appeal to Kim Il Sung six times. Later an officer from the government threatened me. "I understand what you are saying, but we do not have time to listen to everyone's complaints. Just be grateful that you are out of prison and can stay with your family."

I went to my son's university and insisted that he be allowed to finish his degree. But the college responded that the son of a criminal was not eligible to attend the university. Dong Chel and I boiled in anger.

Now I truly knew that in North Korea, the higher officers enjoyed their lives at the cost of the suffering of others.

The Worn Papers

Because my son was no longer in engineering school, he tried to earn some income by repairing electrical wiring. He went to one of the small villages in the countryside.

While he was there, he saw some students from the university who were required to help the farmers in the summer. The farmers are short of hands at that time.

Dong Chel began working with the students. He noticed some students who worked harder than the others. They kept to themselves and disappeared every night.

While he worked alongside these students, he noticed that they kept secretly passing papers to each other. He was curious so he asked, "Why don't you give me one of those, too?"

They flatly denied that they even had such a paper, but later they told him, "We aren't going to give it to you."

After awhile, my son told these students that I had just been released from prison. They must have decided that it was safe to give him some of the pages. He saw that the edges were worn and the words were written differently than the way people speak. The papers had been passed among many North Korean college students.

My son brought home three pages. "Why don't you read this?" he asked me. "I have never seen this kind of writing before. The students said that if you read the words, the truth will set you free."

I read the pages three times, but I didn't pay much attention to what they said.

The Plans We Made

Soon, my son also began to realize that the doctrine of Kim Il Sung was false. We discussed trying to escape from North Korea, but he was worried about what would happen to his father if we left. The government was severe with family members of defectors who were left behind. However, we were unable to locate him. Dong Chel asked, "Mother, how can we go when we do not know what happened to father?"

I told Dong Chel that for his future we must escape from North Korea.

In January 1993, a North Korean spy named In Mo Lee was arrested in South Korea. Amazingly, the South Korean government sent him back to North Korea without hurting him. I thought, *South Korea must be a country where human rights and freedom are protected.* I began to make plans to escape to South Korea.

I met a lady who managed a grocery department. When I confided in her, she advised me to carry out my plans. She told me that when she went on a business trip to Europe, she saw many products made in South Korea in the stores. She said that the Korean products were of higher quality than the European products.

My son and I confirmed our decision to defect to South Korea. But we couldn't cross directly from North Korea to South Korea because of the guarded Demilitarized Zone. To get more details about how to get to South Korea, my son set up a radio. After 11 p.m., we turned out all the lights and got under a blanket to listen to a South Korean radio program. We found one called "My Experience in Seoul." The program described how North Koreans who defect live in South Korea. We also heard Christian radio broadcasting which told us an unknown mystery about God's love and providence and that we can be free in Him. It must have been God who allowed our fingers to turn the knob to that Christian station.

The more we listened, the more anxious we were for the Tumen River to freeze over. Our plan was to walk across the frozen Tumen River, the border between North Korea and China. The river is located on the northern tip of North Korean land. Onsung, near the East coast, is a four-hour walk to the border.

Dong Chel went outside and patrolled the border. When the river had frozen solidly enough, we began preparing to leave. He wanted to take the papers that he had gotten from the university students. I disagreed. "You know, by taking this, we will be in trouble if we get caught. If the guards stop us, we can say we were just trying to get food. That will be our only chance. We cannot take the papers."

I burned the three pages. But before I did, I read them once more. After I arrived in South Korea, I began to read the Bible and discovered that those three pages are from the Bible.

On February 21, 1994, my son ran into the house and told me that this was the day we must leave. It was windy and sleeting. I hesitated to go out on such a cold day, but Dong Chel said, "This is the day heaven has prepared for us to leave North Korea." At five o'clock in the evening, we finally left our house.

Although I resented this land that had caused me so much pain, it was still my homeland. My heart was filled with grief about leaving it. I was an only child. My parents had loved me and told me that I was worth more than many sons in other families. *No one will bring flowers to my parents' graves,* I thought. *Mother and Father, I will return when this nation is unified.*

Because it was a holiday, there weren't many people on the street. We walked on the road to the mountain and then climbed up the steep sides. We gripped trees as we pushed ourselves up the mountainside. We slipped down many times.

Finally, we stood on top of the 500-meter (1,640-foot) summit. We were out of breath from our climb as well as our fear. Fortunately, the day was cloudy and the many trees hid our bodies.

After catching our breath, we ran down the other side of the mountain. I could see the ice on the Tumen River brightly reflecting the moonlight. When we neared the river bank, I told my son, "You listen to me. I will walk behind you. If a soldier spots us, only I will get shot.

We ran down the mountain. The ice of the Tumen River was brightly reflecting the moonlight.

You must run without looking back. You must survive and live in the free country."

We arrived at the river's bank. Swoosh! Something broke the silence. Two birds flew loudly into the sky. My heart stopped for a second. At that moment, my son noticed a North Korean soldier's bunker. God even used birds to caution us. Suddenly he grabbed me and we ran across the Tumen River, arriving on the other side in record time. We hid behind big rocks and looked back at the North Korean side of the river. Everything was still. I thought, *The guards must not have been watching the empty, frozen river because it was so cold and windy.*

Escape to South Korea

In the dark before the sun came up, my son and I decided to go to an apartment I had visited once ten years ago. When I was the commercial chief, I did business with a Korean Chinese man whose last name was Kim. I thought he might be willing to help us escape to South Korea. Even as we crossed the Tumen River, I felt as if someone were holding my hand and leading me to Mr. Kim's house.

When we arrived at the apartment complex, I didn't remember which building Mr. Kim lived in and which door I should knock on. By this time, it was two o'clock in the morning.

My son anxiously asked me, "Mother, are you sure you can find the house you visited ten years ago? In ten years, even the mountains change. To me, all the apartments look the same!"

As he cried, I became more nervous. Yet I felt something leading me by the hand. Finally, I stood before a door and knocked on it. Amazingly, I heard a sleepy voice—it was the one I had heard ten years ago!

Tears poured down my face. This was an unbelievable miracle! Although I didn't realize it then, God must have provided a miracle through His grace.

Mr. Kim opened the door, but tried to shut it immediately because he thought he was seeing a ghost. Someone had told him I was dead. I was also extremely worn out and had a very tired, gaunt face. When I explained who I was, he was surprised and welcomed us in. As we talked, he encouraged us to go to South Korea. We stayed in his home until morning when we went to the train station. We decided to go to Heilongjiang Province, which is located on the eastern side of China.

The people in Heilongjiang Province saved our lives. They sympathize with the suffering of the North Koreans and wanted to help us get safely to South Korea. I cannot write about all the places my son and I stayed or the names of the people who helped us out because I am afraid that the North Korean government will harm them.

Thirteen days after my son and I crossed the Tumen River, North Korean police came to Heilongjiang Province searching for us. I saw wanted posters with pictures of me and my son stuck on the walls of shops and train stations. I even saw them at the train station in Beijing as we traveled by train. Inspections for all travelers tightened. My son and I changed our clothes to disguise ourselves and escaped to Hong Kong.

We experienced another miracle at the Hong Kong border. Twenty travelers, including us, had counterfeit resident identification. Before we crossed the border from China, the police checked everyone's papers very carefully. They arrested every illegal person except my son and me. A customer service officer called out, "They have real identification papers."

When I think of it now, this couldn't have happened if God had not been working.

New Customs, New Ideas

In December 1995, we finally arrived in South Korea. It had taken us a year and ten months to defect. The first few months, we were protected by the South Korean government. During that time, we were debriefed.

One day, an inspector came to ask me a few questions. His smile and his gentleness were so different from what I had experienced in North Korea. As he sat down he said, "Today I would normally be in church, but I was assigned to talk to you."

I didn't know what he meant when he mentioned church.

He continued, 'If you want to adjust quickly to living in South Korea by forgetting all your suffering, you should read this book." He pulled out a thick, black book. I didn't know what it was. I later learned it was a Bible.

He opened it. Each page was filled with black letters. Then he began to sing *Amazing Grace*.

I knew the tune and followed him in singing.

He stopped, shocked that I knew the song since I came from a land that recognized no god. "How do you know that song?" he asked me. "Where did you learn it?"

I didn't know myself where I had learned the song. I had no recollection of ever singing it. I asked him if I could see his song book. I opened the book to another song and I was able to sing it, too. I knew the tune! But I still didn't have any recollection of learning such music.

This puzzled me, so I kept thinking about it. I began to read the black book the man had given me. As I was reading, I came to Exodus 14. I remembered seeing those words on the pages my son had brought home from the students who were working in the fields. It is the story of Moses and the people crossing the Red Sea. God used a pillar of fire at night and a cloud during the day to lead His people.

I kept reading the Bible. Every time I read, I knew it wasn't me who brought me this far but some other Power who allowed me to escape from prison and North Korea.

Then I began to remember things from when I was very young. My mother and her friends would close the front door and do embroidery work together and sing from time to time. Sometimes her friends would stay all night and sing about going to heaven. I remembered their faces. They had such joy. I also recalled how my mother would lull me to sleep. She would carry me on her back and pat me while she sang to me. Some of these songs were hymns, including *Amazing Grace*.

At times, my mother and grandmother had said to me, "Soon Ok, anywhere you go, even to the place where there are no people deep in the mountain or on top of the rocks, no one can touch the hairs of your head. The animals cannot even touch you. When you ask heaven, you will be given what you ask." I did not know then what they meant. Yet all these things remained in the back of my mind throughout my life.

Later, I realized that my grandmother and my mother had been telling me the Word of God in a safe way. In North Korea, Christian parents do not tell their children about God because the Communists try to get children to report Christian parents to the Party. When the children go to school, the teachers ask them if their parents ever secretly read out of a black book. The children are promised honor if they report their parents. But when the children tell on their parents, the parents are taken away. Therefore, parents are very careful about what they tell their children.

Before she died, my mother had asked me not to practice any ancestry worship. I followed her wish, but I never knew why she wanted this. Now I was beginning to understand her beliefs.

Real Freedom

While we were in Heilongjiang Province in China, a Korean Chinese family enabled me to see the love of God. Their house was very near a church. In fact, I must have passed by the front of the church many times. In North Korea, I was determined to avoid anything spiritual because I was afraid I would be killed for believing in any spirit. I was also very scared about being possessed by a spirit, and I classified Christians as people who are possessed by a spirit. I could not distinguish the difference between God and spirits.

However, the lady of the house where we stayed had been paralyzed for many years. Her husband had given up a lot to try to treat her by taking her to many doctors and hospitals. They were unable to help her. But when she accepted Jesus Christ a few years later, she was healed. I could not even tell that she was once half paralyzed. Her husband also accepted Jesus as his Lord. This couple fed my son and me; they gave us clothes to wear and a place to rest. Most importantly, almost every day they prayed for our safe trip to South Korea. We were not related to them, and they didn't even know us. Yet, they kept us in their house when they knew very well that they could be severely penalized if the Chinese Public Security Bureau found out that they were keeping North Koreans.

I began to wonder, *Why are these people doing this for us?* It did not take long to understand the reason. I knew they were doing this because they really wanted me to become a child of God.

On the way to South Korea, my son and I had many difficulties. We had no money, no food, and no place to stay. Unconsciously, I murmured for help. Though I didn't kneel down and pray, God answered and provided our needs miraculously.

I attended church the first week I was released after my debriefing with the South Korean official. As the preacher began to preach, he seemed to be talking only to me. He said, "You must read the Bible to have a good life."

So for selfish reasons and with curiosity, I began to read the Bible. I wanted to be blessed and to have a good life. I read in the car, in the train on the way to speak about the plight of North Korean prisoners, and at home whenever I found time. In the beginning, I really wanted to be blessed materially because the pastor said the book contains the truth on how to live richly. As I was reading, I did not find what the pastor said, but as I read more, I began to understand what he really meant. When I read in John 8:32 that "the truth will set you free," I wanted to believe the God of my mother and grandmother and commit my life to Christ to have real *freedom*. Soon my son also accepted Jesus and began to come to church with me without grumbling.

Chapter 20

I Will Never Forget

WITHIN SEVEN MONTHS, MY SON AND I had found a small home to start our new lives. Since I had lived only in a Communist country, I had to adjust to a capitalistic, democratic system. It is not easy to live with freedom and have freedom to choose. I now have to select what color of clothes I will wear and what type of food I will eat. It is rich man's complaint. I still have much pain from the torture I received in the North Korean prisons.

My son first entered the university to finish his engineering degree. Then he switched to studying Chinese so he could go to China and evangelize North Koreans. His desire is to return to North Korea to tell of God's love or work with ministries that bring the gospel to North Korea.

Some time after we arrived in South Korea, I learned that my husband had been sent to a certain prison in North Korea. I later learned that he was no longer at that prison. I am pretty sure that he is no longer living. He was a good teacher who was innocent. It was only because of me that he went to prison. He was a victim of the godless Communist system. It is my prayer that if he is alive, he will also be protected by the power of God until we meet again when the Korean nation is unified.

When I left North Korea, I had two missions: to tell the world about the human abuse in North Korea and to bring my son back to North Korea when the nation is unified and to take revenge on those who persecuted me and destroyed my family. But after I found the joy of knowing Jesus Christ, I changed my attitude and now have two other missions: to ask Christians around the world to pray for the persecuted people in North Korea and to make my son's wish to study to be a Christian missionary in North Korea come true.

The Mission

Whenever I can, I go to churches to tell of the situation in North Korea. When people say it is difficult to evangelize North Korea, I tell them that if we pray to God and follow His assistance, we can bring the gospel into North Korea. Many of the people there are hungry and dying, but now that I know the God of heaven and His Son Jesus Christ, I think it is more important to send the Scriptures than to send rice. We must bring God's love and His Word to them to help them even more.

The North Korean people do not know anything about God. Yet there are some things we can do to help them know. When I lived in North Korea, a customs officer had confiscated items that people were bringing across the border from China. One was a little sack containing perfume samples. The samples were wrapped in paper that had a cross on it.

Since North Koreans don't have many possessions, they don't throw anything away. Even if a piece of paper had a cross on it, a North Korean wouldn't throw it away. A high-level official in the Party wanted to carry it in his pocket to smell good.

Another time, I saw a strange picture on some material that had been confiscated. When I came to South Korea, I learned that the picture was of Jesus. People will keep this material with the picture on it even though they know it's illegal to have the picture; they will not give it back to the government because they have nothing. We can use many ways to help the North Koreans learn about God.

When I first began to testify of the brutality in North Korea, no one believed me. Someone told me, "No way! How could people survive in such an environment!"

Perhaps it is natural that people who have not suffered like this think I'm exaggerating, but I am sad to admit that this is true and is happening right now. I don't expect anyone to tell me they understand what I'm trying to describe. No one can understand except the people who were there with me.

I used to have dreams every night. In my dreams, I saw myself being tortured by a man. I saw a man tied to a post waiting to be shot. I saw the prisoners straining to finish their quotas. I saw my friends who were not allowed to be human anymore watching me walk out of prison. How could I ever forget them until the day I die? I know they will live within my sad heart forever.

However, I have been healed with the love of God and His comfort. I no longer dream dreadful dreams. I am free.

Someone asked me, "What are the most gratifying things for you in South Korea?"

I answered without hesitation, "I am so thankful to God who brought me to love Him."

However, the forgotten people in North Korea are the ones we should pray for and send God's love. We should also remember those believers who are in prison because they will not deny the God in heaven. Their pleading eyes cry out to us. We must be faithful to bring God's love to them all.

RESOURCES

Other Books by Living Sacrifice Book Company

Tortured for Christ: 30th Anniversary Edition
Pastor Richard Wurmbrand
This dramatic testimony shocked the Western world. After spending years in underground prison cells and solitary confinement, enduring inhumane tortures, Richard and Sabina Wurmbrand emerged with the testimony of today's Christian martyrs. The new 30th Anniversary Edition features photos, testimonies from Christian leaders, and an update on the work of The Voice of the Martyrs. (Paperback, 176 pp., $6.00)

In God's Underground
Pastor Richard Wurmbrand
This inspiring drama speaks of God's comfort to Christians imprisoned for their faith by hard-line Communists. Sentenced to "life" in a death room, these faithful believers were able to rejoice in their Lord amid the most horrific conditions. It is a story of triumphant faith. (Paperback, 276 pp., $7.00)

Victorious Faith
Pastor Richard Wurmbrand
Sail from tribulation into the peace-giving waters of Christian faith and testimony. A voyage certain to refresh and inspire every person confronted with suffering. (Paperback, 128 pp., $6.00)

With God in Solitary Confinement
Pastor Richard Wurmbrand
He was alone for three years in a prison cell—30 feet below the ground. During that time, Richard Wurmbrand never saw the sun, touched the grass, or glanced at another human being. However, as he sat shackled and alone, he heard a very clear voice—Christ ministering to him, His

voice never fading. What resulted was a man full of the love of Jesus Christ, wanting to proclaim all that God had spoken during those years of total intimacy. This book holds those proclamations of great joy from a solitary cell. (Paperback, 192 pp., $7.00)

Between Two Tigers
Compiled by Tom White
From forbidden baptisms and secret meetings to imprisonment, Christians in Vietnam pay a great price for their faith in Christ. Caught between Communist police and tribal religions, their many victories are evidence of God's faithfulness. *Between Two Tigers* is a collection of testimonies from today's persecuted Christians in Vietnam. (Paperback, 192 pp., $8.00)

God's Missiles Over Cuba
Tom White
Behind the "Sugar Cane Curtain," an American Christian faces a 24-year prison sentence for "undermining" Cuba's Communist system—with gospel tracts! Tom White's true-life account of his imprisonment, the brutal treatment that followed, and his introduction to Cuba's living martyrs. (Paperback, 222 pp., $6.00)

Juche: A Christian Study of North Korea's State Religion
Thomas J. Belke
This book takes you on a journey into North Korea to view what is possibly the most rigidly controlling religious system on the planet—Juche. Under the Juche belief system, man is proclaimed God in a nation whose government has officially decided against Christianity for all of its citizens. The majority of North Koreans today have never heard the name of Jesus. In this book, the author explores Juche's origins, central teachings, and spiritual dimension, as well as a biblical view of its future. (Paperback, 418 pp., $15.00)

Videos by The Voice of the Martyrs

Faith Under Fire
Faith Under Fire features interviews with Christians who face persecution head-on. You will meet a Muslim whose "road to Damascus" conversion leads to his persecution; a Chinese pastor suffering under the

"strike-hard" policy that Christians now face; and a Vietnamese teenager dealing with her father's arrest and imprisonment for his work in the underground church. *Faith Under Fire* will challenge you to consider, "Is my faith ready to hold up under fire?" (Contains dramatic scenes that may not be suitable for children.)

Stephen's Test of Faith (*children's video*)
Twelve-year-old Stephen is mocked and ridiculed for his faith. That night in a dream, Stephen travels through history meeting Jesus, Stephen the martyr, families about to enter the Roman coliseum, William Tyndale, Christian children in today's Middle East, and others who dare to share their faith.

Filmed internationally, *Stephen's Test* is an inspiring challenge to all ages, a powerful tool for Sunday school, the unsaved, classrooms, your home. This walk with faithful heroes encourages us with their historical call to continue following Jesus Christ when we are put to "the test." (Includes study outline with Scripture references.)

The Voice of the Martyrs has available many other books, videos, brochures, and other products to help you learn more about the persecuted church. In the U.S., to request a resource catalog, order materials, or receive our free monthly newsletter, call (800) 747-0085 or write to:

> The Voice of the Martyrs
> P.O. Box 443
> Bartlesville, OK 74005-0443

If you are in Canada, Australia, England, or New Zealand, contact:

> The Voice of the Martyrs
> P.O. Box 117
> Port Credit
> Mississauga, Ontario L5G 4L5
> Canada

> Release International
> P.O. Box 19
> Bromley BR2 9TZ
> England

> The Voice of the Martyrs
> P.O. Box 598
> Penrith NSW 2751
> Australia

> The Voice of the Martyrs
> P.O. Box 69-158
> Glendene, Auckland 1230
> New Zealand